DEJUNK YOUR LIFE

DEJUNK YOUR LIFE

Helen Foster

AURUM PRESS

This edition first published 2002 by
Aurum Press Limited, 25 Bedford Avenue,
London WC1B 3AT

Produced by Essential Books

Project Editor: Emma Dickens
Designers: Barbara Saulini, Sibashan Chetty

Text Editors: Sarah Hulbert, Janet Law

Page 28, "How Much Does Your Clutter Cost You?" reprinted with permission
from the Clean Team website - www.thecleanteam.com
page 111, "Tim and Dierdre" case study adapted from "Balanced Lives" with
permission from New Ways to Work
page 112, "Term Time Working" adapted from "Changing Work Patterns for Men"
with permission from New Ways to Work
page 115, "Heather" case study reprinted from "Working from Home" from New
Ways to Work with permission from the NatWest Group

A catalogue record for this book is available from the British Library.

ISBN 1 85410 858 1

Cover by Neal Townsend for Essential Books

Contents

Introduction

What Does Dejunk Mean?

Dejunking is a way of getting what you want in life. It's not especially complicated, it's not at all technical, but it works. The idea behind dejunking is simple – if your life is too complex and too full, by simplifying those areas that don't fulfil you, you can make space for those that will. Simple, eh?

The truth is that most of us have too much in our lives. Just look at how many things we try to do each day. It's no wonder that 77 per cent of people say they feel they've lost control of their lives. It's also no wonder that we don't know how to deal with that. A recent study by London's Institute of Optimum Nutrition looked directly at how people coped with stress. It found that 54 per cent of people were not coping. Increasingly we feel we are unable to control the world we live in – our work, our money, our relationships and even the homes that are supposed to be our sanctuaries. Dissatisfaction with our quality of life is at an all-time high, and our sometimes fatalistic natures ensure that we believe changing things is beyond our grasp.

One reason is that, for such a small word, change signifies huge restructure – if I called this book "Change Your Life" you'd probably have a definite image of what it's about. People who've given up their high-flying, high-finance jobs to run cheese farms or who've swapped their chrome-filled loft apartments for thatched cottages with a view of the hills. Changing your life entails big differences and big sacrifices and that's something that many of us can't face or can't be bothered to deal with. Dejunking, however, uses simple steps to create change. In simple terms, dejunking allows your life to become less complex and more focused – it's streamlining the way you act, the way you think and what you do to ensure that you get what you want from your life. Even the tiniest changes will make differences.

Later in this book you'll meet Susanna, a woman who has changed her life focus, her relationships and her entire self-image simply by clearing the clutter in her home. You'll also encounter a man who's changing his career because he started exercising and a woman who believes she saved her marriage by changing her diet. To me, these people sum up the first rule of dejunk – that no positive action is too small to make a difference to your life – and that it's often the little things that can make the biggest differences. Taking one positive step can lead to things spiralling out of control – even thinking about what you want is enough to start things off. "What you believe is how you'll live," says psychology expert Robert Holden. "Change what you believe and you can change your life." Sometimes change is immediate, sometimes it takes time, but only by putting things in motion can changes happen. In a nutshell, dejunking is simplifying the chaos in our lives in order to create change. It's about taking control and using that control to make what you want of your life.

Why Dejunk Now?

We need to dejunk if we're going to be happy. Our lives have become paradoxical. We eat bad food because we don't have time to cook. We feel stressed but are under too much pressure to relax. And when we do have time off we're too tired to enjoy it. Many areas in our life are contributing to this situation.

OUR JOBS

The hours that we work now are longer than ever before. The average person in the UK is putting in a forty-four-hour week, in the USA the annual average working time has increased by the equivalent of a month since the 1970s. "Yet our lives are so much more insecure than ever before," says Professor Cary Cooper from the University of Manchester Institute of Science and Technology. "Despite asking us to work harder and work longer, our employers are not rewarding us with the job security that we expect for such a commitment and this causes internal conflicts, illness and other problems."

58 per cent of people are tired all the time

At any one time, a quarter of men and a third of women in the UK feel "fed-up"

35 per cent of couples argue at least once a week – most commonly about money

50 per cent of people would swap a day's pay for a day off but don't think they can afford to

62 per cent of adults want to simplify their lives but don't know how to start

Dejunking your life can solve all these problems and more

TECHNOLOGY

Using technology to simplify our lives has not helped things – it has made things worse. Advances like e-mail, "call waiting" and mobile phones ensure that we can never switch off from any part of our life. "And we are expected to produce instant responses," says Cary Cooper. "The result is that we're running ourselves as an instant society. Instead of taking the long-term view of stress control through exercise or taking time out to keep calm, we're taking the fast-track, using alcohol or cigarettes to create instant gratification." The long-term view no longer fits into our lives or society and so we find it hard to incorporate it into our lives.

CONSUMERISM

On average, Americans spend a year of their lives watching adverts on the TV, and British teenagers have seen 150,000 ads by the time they reach eighteen. The result is the "disease" of "affluenza" – no matter what you spend, it's never enough – which is epidemic in society today. We own more possessions now than ever before. "If you compare your home with that of your grandparents you'd discover you possess about a third more items," says San Francisco-based personal organizer Allison Van Norman. "Yet you probably care about a smaller percentage. We now live in a disposable world. The things we buy are purchased to fulfil an emotional need to own things but they don't actually give us any pleasure. The clutter with which we surround ourselves just creates mess and stifles our life."

OUR HEALTH

The number of pollutants that we subject ourselves to now is immense. Two-thirds of the calories we take in every day are from foods containing substances the nutritionist Patrick Holford refers to as "anti-nutrients" (foods that take more nutrients to process than they actually provide). In one year we consume 200 million alcoholic drinks and smoke 83 billion cigarettes. Add this to the damage caused by the stress and strains that we are under and you have a society founded on sickness.

OUR RELATIONSHIPS

Even our relationships and family life are not fulfilling us. More couples than ever are divorcing and, according to a survey by Relate, over 45 per cent of arguments are about time, work or money. "The fact that we have to distance ourselves from feelings regarding our working lives is having effects on our emotional lives," says relationships psychologist Susan Quilliam. "Women particularly are suppressing how they really feel and this is also occurring in their relationships. This female suppression combined with men's increasing willingness to talk about things that worry them is causing conflict – and it's not conflict that we feel we have time to deal with. Even as recently as ten years ago relationships always came first over work, especially for women. Now things are on a more equal footing, and that can mean things that are going wrong get ignored – or at least pushed aside."

We're in a mess and we're rapidly beginning to learn that the only people who are going to be able to get us out of it are ourselves.

At Last, Some Good News

From reading the above you may well be thinking that things have got so bad we're never going to sort them out. Well, that's not true, there has never been a better time to start dejunking your life. Many people are starting to do that right now. Gerald Celente of the Trends Research Institute in Rhinebeck, New York, links this change in attitude to the baby-boomer generation reaching their forties and fifties. According to him, they are adopting the mantra, "We want to do what we want to do", and they are following through by doing just that.

Living the dejunked life is also a natural progression for non-baby-boomers. In fact, it's the way future predictors believe society is going to head as we enter the twenty-first century. In the late 1970s, trends expert Faith Popcorn predicted something she called "cocooning". It described the way our lives were becoming more home-based and internalized due to the world outside becoming just too big, too full and too scary. Just like our Neanderthal ancestors, we started retreating to our "caves". In the early 1990s, Popcorn described how cocooning had progressed. She revealed that we were becoming even more entrenched. Now, not only were we withdrawing physically from the outside world, we were withdrawing emotionally, spending less time on people-contact generally and ensuring that those people we did surround ourselves with were those we truly cared about. In the future, Popcorn believed, we'd take this withdrawal even further and we'd live lives where everything that didn't have a use or give us pleasure would be eliminated or at least pared down.

Predictions like this mean a lot for all of us. There's a term in nuclear physics, "critical mass", that defines the minimum amount of radioactive material necessary to produce a nuclear reaction. Once critical mass has been reached, the process becomes self-sustaining and the reaction can continue under its own steam. Critical mass has been adopted by the marketing industry as a term to define the level of acceptance that a product or movement needs for it to be absorbed into the public consciousness. The critical mass for dejunking is growing, and soon it's will be an accepted way of life. Sociologist Edward de Bono goes as far as to say that we should set up an Institute for Simplicity – a group of people dedicated to dejunking society.

All around us, the seeds for a dejunked life are being sown. In the last few years many books have been written on a subject called "downshifting". When you downshift, you simplify your life to get away from all the stress and pressure that the world throws at you, day in, day out. It usually involves learning to survive on less money and coming to terms with less status. Laughably, what we have been using to create our own perfect environment is almost a reflection of what got us there in the first place. In the last ten years business has been downshifting on a global scale.

Companies have learnt to get by on less money, to function with fewer resources – and those left behind have paid the price. The truth is that downshifting doesn't work for everyone – it may not be suited to our personalities or our goals – and, let's face it, on a massive scale it's just not feasible for all of us to drop out. At present, over 4 million people (7.8 per cent of the UK population) move to the country every year. If everyone else who claimed this was their dream followed suit, our rural areas would see an influx of millions of people. We'd just create cities with better scenery. If we are going to survive in a world that is becoming more pressurized and more stressful we need to find a system that doesn't involve us all opting out. Instead, we must find a way to adapt our respective environments to allow everyone to get what they want. That system is dejunking.

Do YOU Need to Dejunk?

Look at the following ten statements. For a few moments, think about each one and determine its relevance to your life. Some of them will immediately click with you – people who've read through them have described "feeling a thwack in the pit of my stomach" or said it was "like meeting someone you know really well but never quite understood – and working out exactly why". Tom, one of the guinea pigs for this book, said, "I just read it and thought, 'Yeah, that makes sense,'" which is probably a very dejunked way of looking at things. If a statement doesn't make an immediate connection with you, just sit and think for a few minutes. Ask if it reflects your life in even the smallest way. If not, that's great, this is one area that you don't have to work on. In fact, it's probably an area of your life that you could learn from, and you should think about why this area of your life works. If none of the statements relate to you, you're either a Zen master or not thinking about this properly.

1 **We use 20 per cent of our possessions 80 per cent of the time**

2 **You're judged by the clothes you wear, not by those left in your closet**

3 **You can't separate your mind and body – if one feels bad, so does the other**

4 **You spend one-third of your life at work – should you really spend that time feeling miserable?**

5 **Money isn't a problem – we just have problems with it**

6 How different would your relationship be if you stopped looking for signs that your partner doesn't love you and started looking for signs that he/she does?

7 You can't choose your family, but you can choose your friends. So why do you have so many you don't like?

8 In a healthy family, each member gives. In this way, each member has the opportunity to receive. Are you getting your fair share?

9 To live well with the world around you, you must live well with the world in your head

10 You only have one life and all that matters is to spend it as happily as possible

What Can You Achieve by Dejunking?

The answer is, "Whatever you want". In fact, you may not even realize where the steps that you're taking are leading. Earlier I spoke about Susanna who started clearing her home and ended up going back to school, breaking out of a bad relationship and re-prioritizing her life to ensure that, whenever she had control of her life, she used it to her advantage. She's not unusual. Many people have either dejunked or want to dejunk – be it a career change or a complete lifestyle transformation. I have met people who have become richer, people who have become poorer, people who have got married and people who have got divorced, but they all have one thing in common – they are happier.

It's even worked on me. When I started on this book I thought I had a pretty dejunked life. I lived in a moderately tidy flat. I had a job I liked, went out five nights a week, never worked late and kept my stress under control (well, at least most of the time). But as I started finding out more and more about living a dejunked life, I realized I hadn't quite got it sussed after all. As I was working on the following chapters, I began to find things that weren't quite right. It started simply: the huge pile of mismatched shoes under the bed and the peeling wallpaper in the kitchen just had to go. It progressed to my hair. I'd been bleached blonde since I was fifteen and swore I'd never go back to my natural colour – but suddenly all the time and money I was spending at the hairdressers seemed to be wasted time and money. So I'm now a natural mouse, saving me about £800 a year which I now spend on those clothes I used to waste energy coveting.

And finally it changed my career. When I was made redundant, I saw it as a blessing. I went freelance, which meant I could do what I wanted to do when I wanted to do it. The fact that I could control my income and my environment made me realize that all I really needed to work was a phone, e-mail and a computer. I realized that where I was didn't matter and I'm now upping sticks and moving to New Zealand with my boyfriend. Dejunking has also made me realize that if I don't like it, I can always come back.

All these changes came about for one simple reason. Dejunking can be an extremely powerful force in your life and the more you read about it the more you recognize its power. You suddenly understand that you are on this earth for a short space of time and if you're not using that time to your best advantage – i.e. doing everything you can to make yourself happy – then you're wasting that time. Dejunking may give you more space, it may give you more time, it may even give you more money, but the most important thing that dejunking can give you is the ability to be what you want to be and do what you want to do. I'm glad I had the chance to find that out. I'm glad I had the chance to work my way through this book as I was writing it and I'm glad that by doing it I can give other people the chance to change things too. I hope you gain as much from it as I have. All of us deserve to be happy. We just need to know where to start.

How to Use This Book

Some of you will have looked at that heading and thought, what is she talking about? Don't you just read it? Actually, it's not that simple. If the first rule of dejunk is that little things mean the most, the second is that only you can dejunk your life. I and all the experts in this book may be able to tell you how but what we cannot do is make that change happen for you. There is an awful lot of practical advice in this book and a lot of little things for you to tick and cross to allow you to find the solutions to your own particular problems. By the end of it you will know: exactly which diet you should be following for optimum health; exactly how much money you can survive on in a month; and even exactly how you could be a millionaire in 30 to 40 years' time, should that be your heart's desire. However, unless you actually put things in motion, none of this is going to make any difference to your life. The first thing I'd say about reading this book is do it with a pencil and a highlighter in your hand. Make notes or highlight points you find interesting. You could even make a list of things to implement in your life, perhaps writing one per day in your diary. Whatever your system, just ensure that if you start it, you stick to it. To make things easier, there's a Summary and an Action Plan at the end of each chapter.

You can read the whole book to get an overview and then go back to the beginning to work through the exercises. You can work through it chapter by chapter and step by step. You can skip to the chapter you believe is most relevant to your life.

Never underestimate the little changes. If you've got a problem with your partner, don't automatically assume that you need the emotional section of this book. Many relationships break down not because there's something wrong with the partnership but because of problems with work, money or external factors, like difficult families. It could be that sorting those out could change things with your partner.

So let's get started. Dejunking your life begins here – you're going to decide what you want from your dejunked life. When you start to change things, you need to make sure that you reap the benefits from what you've achieved. Many people may start a programme like this and then not know how to proceed with it (during my dejunking epiphany, I cleared out my entire kitchen and now have seven empty cupboards and no idea what to put in them). I don't want your life to become the equivalent of my kitchen cupboards, so your first job is to make your wish list.

On a piece of a paper make a list of forty things you want to do in your life. They can be large things – such as improving your relationship or reducing the amount of work you do by 40 per cent – or they could be smaller things – like going to Rome or eating in a certain restaurant. As you work through the book and start to achieve things, use whatever you've gained to "treat" yourself to something from your list. Not only will this help you to keep working through the programme, it can also show you what a difference dejunking can make to your life – and how much fun you can have doing it. If you get to the end of the list, make another one. Remember that life is what you make it – and it's now your job to make it as good as possible.

Chapter 1
Dejunk Your Surroundings

AT THE CURRENT MOMENT, right as you are reading this, someone, somewhere, is looking for something they've lost. It's probably nothing major – car keys or a bill that needs to be paid – but in total they'll spend over a year of their life searching for it, and stuff like it, over and over again. We live in an age of clutter, an age in which we no longer judge ourselves on who we are but on what we possess and we can never reach the stage of believing enough is enough.

It's estimated that there are about 9.7 billion cubic feet of home storage space in the United States and at least a billion in the United Kingdom, and that in both countries 80 per cent of this is filled with stuff we rarely, if ever, use. It's got to the stage where not only is it impossible to be too rich or too thin – you cannot have too much space.

What Effect Does This Have?

First, it wastes time. We spend a lot more time than we realize cleaning up our homes. That doesn't just mean vacuuming and dusting. It means moving homeless junk from room to room. It means endlessly piling up the stack of magazines in the corner of the lounge after we've tried to read the one from the middle, and it means sorting out the pile of clothes that need ironing every time we need something to wear. Experts estimate that if we all dejunked our homes we'd cut the amount of cleaning time we need by 40 per cent – that's an extra 26 minutes a day to yourselves: over a year, it's practically a week. And the more clutter we have the more time we're going to waste. Junk attracts junk; we're not going to care about throwing another newspaper on a pile of twenty. The more clutter we have, the more we create.

Those who think negatively are often surrounded by clutter. "People with extreme depression tend to hoard things," says London-based Feng Shui practitioner Gill Hale. "People going through divorce tend to surround themselves with possessions from the past as protection. Collecting clutter is like an animalistic reflex to us. We're hurt, we're wounded and we have to hide." However, it's also true that those who are surrounded by clutter tend to feel more negative about themselves. According to the principles of Feng Shui, this happens because the clutter restricts the flow of *chi*, the essential energy that surrounds us all, and unless that *chi* is released we cannot get the most from our lives.

Clutter also has negative physical effects. Experts believe that people who work in untidy offices suffer more stress than those in tidy environments. The constant mislaying of car keys or kids' schoolbooks leaves us in a perpetual state of lateness and hence stress. Add this to the fact that allergy experts believe our inability to throw things away has increased the dust levels in our homes – and this could be contributing to the threefold increase in asthma cases over the last twenty years – and you can see that clutter doesn't just make for an untidy house. It makes for an unhealthy body and mind too.

So What Happens When You Start to Dejunk?

The results of moving clutter are far greater than having a tidier-looking home or keys you can find at a moment's notice. Clutter experts believe that by dejunking your surroundings physically you can develop a higher mental state. "Being surrounded by clutter keeps you mired in the past," says US-based organizer Allison Van Norman. "The clients I see that are surrounded by junk are extremely fuzzy about their present and their future. They don't know what to do with their job or their relationship, but as you dejunk, things become clearer. It's like they reveal what's been hidden."

Susanna, a medical researcher from San Francisco, agrees. "I had been brought up in a family where you weren't taught to throw things away and I had never cleared anything out. I was terrified of what was in those cupboards and boxes – applications to schools I never went to but wished I had, pictures from relationships that hadn't worked out. These were areas of my life that I blamed for what was going wrong in my life now and I didn't want to have to face up to them."

Eventually Susanna began to work with Allison Van Norman and they cleared out everything she had hoarded for the last ten years. "I met Allison at a time when I was trying to get things clear in my head. I was in a bad relationship, I was having problems organizing my time and I wasn't fulfilled

Simplify Your Life

Our environment, our looks and our bodies are among the easiest things in the world to dejunk and they can produce amazing results:

Cutting clutter can decrease the amount of time you spend maintaining your home by 40 per cent

Organizing your wardrobe can decrease the time it takes you to get ready in the morning by 50 per cent

Improving levels of just one vitamin in your diet can cut sick days by 34 per cent

People with a professional image are 65 per cent more likely to get promoted than scruffy dressers

75 per cent of people on an optimum eating plan reported more energy

in my job and I didn't know what to do. Clearing things physically just seemed like a good way to start but as I went through everything, I faced up to a lot, I got some perspective and began to see what I wanted more clearly. It's taken a year, but I'm now in a relationship that works for me, I'm going back to school and I've made more time for myself. Once the obstacles you've always claimed were holding you back have gone, there's nothing to stop you getting on in your life – and in my case, clearing up my surroundings was what it took to start that process happening."

How to Get Started

The bad news is, you are unlikely to dejunk your clutter in an hour. Depending on how much junk you have, it could take a day, a solid week or even longer – it will also always take at least twice as long as you think it will. The key to a successful dejunk, therefore, is to give it the time it needs. Now this doesn't mean you book vacation time to get to grips with your mess (although it could be the best week you've ever spent); instead, you need to fit your task to your time. If you've got an hour, do a drawer, two hours a closet and so on. It doesn't matter how big the space you decide to tackle is, what counts is that you complete the task. Half-finished dejunks create more mess than they eliminate.

The D.E.J.U.N.K. Rules

No matter how small or large the space you're clearing, the rules remain the same. You travel armed with six receptacles – cardboard boxes are best as they can either be stacked or disposed of. When you enter your chosen space you must go through every item and define it in one of the six ways below. Only handle things once: You're never going to finish this thing if you move stuff from box to box. Once it's in a box, it's gone.

Dumpable: It's rubbish. It's no good to you. It's no good to anyone else. Throw it away!

Essentials: These are the items you use regularly at least every month or two. When you come across an essential item, ask yourself if it is in the best place. If not, determine where is best and put it there now – but before you close the cupboard, count up how many versions of this item you own. If you live alone, do you really need twelve cups? Would your life really suffer if you whittled them down to four? Think realistically how many identical items you need and eliminate the rest – and all the cleaning and maintenance that go with them.

J **umble**: You haven't used it for a year and you're not going to use it in the next six months – but it's too good to throw away. This box is going to friends, to charity or to a car boot sale.

U **ndecided**: If it takes you more than five seconds to decide what to do with an item, put it in this box. When it's full, tape the box up and date it. Store it in the loft or similar. If after one year you haven't had an occasion to go into the box and retrieve an item, it goes unopened to either the charity shop or the rubbish dump. Just one thing to remember – if you also store useful things in the loft, label these boxes with what's in them or come December you'll end up opening your undecided boxes to find the decorations.

N **ostalgia**: Anything you are sentimentally attached to goes in here. This box can get big, so use the container principle: decide how much space you want to allocate to sentimental items before you start dejunking. Find a container of that size and once it's full, that's it – something has to come out before another piece can go in.

K **aput**: If the only reason you're not using something is because it's broken, put it in this box. At the end of the dejunk, take everything to be fixed within one week or throw it away. If it's not mended by then, it never will be.

Yes, you have to be ruthless, but that's the only way you're going to dejunk your clutter. If the whole thing seems completely overwhelming, prioritize. Allison Van Norman suggests spending a week determining where the problems lie in your home

How Long Should You Keep Things For?

One problem when you're dejunking is deciding how long you actually need to keep things. More often than not, we keep bills or receipts "just in case" but the case never comes. Here, therefore, are the rules for what to keep for how long:

WAGE SLIPS: Three months if you're employed by a company; six years if you're self-employed

P60'S AND TAX RETURNS: Five years

UTILITY BILLS: One year – especially if you pay on a budget scheme

BANK STATEMENTS/CREDIT CARD BILLS: Six months

RECEIPTS: Until the credit card statement comes in or the guarantee runs out. You should also keep receipts for very expensive items with your insurance details to eliminate hold-ups in the event of a claim

IF YOU ARE SELF-EMPLOYED: Anything to do with your business should be kept for six years

Now you've cleared out the clutter, all that should be left in your home are things that benefit your life either practically or aesthetically. One of the following is likely to have happened:

1 Everything's perfectly put away; your cupboards are tidy and all is well

2 You've now got loads of empty cupboard space and nothing to put in it, in which case, start to look around and see what else you can clear up

3 You're still feeling cluttered. The truth is, most of us have sufficient storage space in our homes, but we have inefficient storage space and so even after we have dejunked we can't put everything away neatly enough. The good news is, maximizing your storage space doesn't have to mean a major overhaul ...

and which affect you the most. Is it an established home for your keys that you need or clothes you can find in five minutes flat? Identify what's really stopping you getting things done and tackle it.

The Dejunked Home

THINK DEAD SPACE: Alcoves, huge cupboards with empty space within them, backs of doors, ceilings, are usually all dead space that can be effectively and attractively used to display items.

THINK JAPANESE: No, not matting and rattan; I mean height. When Tokyo realized it didn't have enough floor space to deal with all the people who needed to be in the area, it didn't decide it needed to live somewhere bigger, it just got taller – and you should do the same with storage.

THINK SURFACES: What's on top of appliances like your washing machine or fridge. If the answer is "nothing", why not? The top of the washer is the perfect place to store the powder; if you can't bear this aesthetically, buy a nicer container – but use the space.

THINK THE SPACE/STORE RATIO: Successful storage works hard. When you buy new furniture check how much it actually holds. A bedside table may be handy for storing lights, but that's it. Instead, learn the space/store ratio: Of every piece of furniture you buy, 75 per cent of the square footage should be able to be used as storage (you don't have to use it, you just want the option).

THINK AESTHETICALLY: While the idea of beautiful open shelving full of beautiful things works well in interiors magazines, it doesn't always work well at home. Only ever allocate open shelving to beautiful things. The food and crockery of the average mortal should be stored behind closed doors.

YOU'RE RIGHT-BRAINED: If you're creative, always late, hate working to a schedule, like thinking of ideas but not necessarily implementing them and have a lot of visual stimuli in your life, you are likely to be a right-brained thinker – and therefore a clutterer. "Right-brain thinkers find it very hard to put things away," says Seattle-based holistic organizer, Lorraine Chalicki. "They think things through visually and if something isn't close by them they find it hard to relate to it, or they forget about it. Filing is extremely hard for them because they don't find it easy to pigeonhole things – they can't narrow something down to one file, they have to have three or four subsets. They're therefore extremely likely to clutter."

YOUR AGE: "Older people who have lived through recessions or depressions are likely to clutter," says Lorraine Chalicki. "There's that 'waste not want not' philosophy that means they physically can't bring themselves to dump things."

YOUR GENDER: Men and women clutter differently. Women tend to buy lots of things and never get round to throwing them out. "Yet when you teach them how, they are happy to dispense with anything useless," says Allison Van Norman. Men, however, actively tend to keep things. "They seem particularly prone to paper – newspapers, bills, tickets from rock concerts – and they hate to throw things away. When I organize the clutter in a man's home he doesn't normally want to lose any of it. He just wants me to compartmentalize things better and then put it all in a closet to hide it. Women want it gone."

YOUR PARENTS: Your upbringing also affects how you clutter. Many people with overtidy parents "rebel" by never clearing up, those with "deprived" upbringings often surround themselves with stuff out of security. Spoilt children have the same problem – they're used to having things given to them

THINK ACCESS: Do not just put things in hard-to-reach areas such as under the bed without a system – you will spend hours trying to find things. It took me two years of trying to find the left shoe of a pair to realize that if I stored the shoes in labelled boxes I could pull out both shoes at once.

RETHINK SPACE CONSTRAINTS: Only in modern times have rooms had to have rigid roles. The Shaker-style portable jug and bowl bathroom next to the bed may not have been luxurious but it certainly took up a lot less space than an en-suite. Don't think of rooms as roles, think of them as spaces.

The Dejunked Office

The average person handles 300 pieces of paper a day and many of them end up in huge piles all over the working environment. The result is chaos and a working day that sees the average paper-pusher spending 22 minutes hunting for lost documents. Over your life this adds up to over a year shuffling bills, business cards and junk mail. Part of the reason for the paper overload is overwork. We don't have enough time to deal with the papers that do matter, let alone to tackle those that don't. However, part of the problem is that, psychologically, we believe that a busy desk is the sign of a busy mind and that by overloading our desk with paper we look as if we are overloaded by work and therefore we are oh-so-important. Sadly, that's not the impression it gives. "Most of the bosses I deal with think busy desks drag down the company and make it look like someone can't cope," says Allison Van Norman. "The professional desk contains those items only immediately applicable to the task at hand –

everything else should be dealt with, dumped or delegated." PS: For those of you who don't work in an office and think this section doesn't actually concern you, can I just mention the gas bill, the bank statement and that pile of junk mail telling you you've won a sandwich toaster that sits by your phone? All of us are under paper attack, it's only the location that differs.

Timesaver Tip: The last-minute clear-up

You've got people coming round, the place is a mess and you haven't the time or inclination to do anything about it. Homes stylist Sarah Lynch offers some suggestions.

• *Make it look brighter. Turn on any lights and, if it's light enough outside, open the curtains as wide as you can. Light rooms always look cleaner than dark ones – no one thinks you're trying to hide anything in a light room.*

• *Stay in one or two areas – close the doors on the rest. Do not feel obliged to give anyone the grand tour.*

• *Clean mirrors and any glass doors, picture windows or glass table tops.*

• *If you haven't got time to wash the dishes, put them in a sink full of suds.*

Three areas to watch out for:

• *The hallway – it gives the first impression so dump last week's newspapers that you're waiting to recycle, any dog-walking shoes and muddy mats.*

• *The bathroom – it's the one area where people really don't want to see any dirt (ditto the kitchen but unless you're eating in there, don't let them in).*

• *The room you're going to be in. Dust surfaces and get rid of any displaced items or piles of paper.*

• *Spray furniture polish just before they come in, they'll associate the smell with a clean house and won't think to look. Never apologize for the mess – why bring it to people's attention?*

The "Deal with it, Delegate it or Dump it" Method of Paper Attack

Not only do we pile our paper or lose bits of paper just to add to the mess (and time we spend dealing with things every day), on average we touch every piece of paper at least five time. The first rule of dejunked paper control is, therefore, touch each piece only once. Whenever a piece of paper arrives on your desk, you should apply one of the three Ds.

How Much Does Your Clutter Cost You?

Storing clutter costs you money. Every penny of your rent or your mortgage pays for something in your home, right? So how much of that money are you paying to store junk? When faced with stubborn "junkies" like you, Jeff Campbell, founder of the Clean Team company and author of *Clutter Control and Speed Cleaning*, tries the following exercise in persuasion:

First calculate how much you're paying for each square foot of your home by dividing the square footage by the monthly rent or mortgage. For example, if you live in a 1,500 sq. ft house and have a $/£1,500 monthly payment, that's obviously £/$1 per square foot per month

Now add up how many square feet you devote to storing things you don't use. Everything should be counted here – shelves, wardrobes, space under the bed. If you have a room or a cupboard you can't use because it's so full, count the whole space, not just the amount actually filled with rubbish

Multipy the sq. ft area by the cost per sq. ft and there you have how much your junk is costing you each month. And if the answer to this exercise is more than 20 per cent of your monthly rent/mortgage, you need to dejunk

DEAL WITH IT

If it's a bill, write the cheque, write the envelope and stick on the stamp ready for mailing. If there's no money in the account, do all of this and stick a Post-It on it saying what day it should go – at least then you won't touch it until payday, and you're less likely to lose it. If it's a letter, draft notes on the top and either write the letter – or delegate it. Unless it's a complicated task, all papers should be dealt with on the day they arrive at your desk or through the mail. Complicated tasks should go in your in-tray and you should book diary time to deal with them every week – okay? Finally, if you're not one of those people who find it therapeutic to go through paperwork, bear in the mind the following. Stress expert Michelle Kay McNabb from Vitalizers says our bodies don't actually function too creatively for the first two hours of a Monday morning workday. Therefore, anything you do at this time is likely to be less impressive than if you had waited until lunchtime. Monday a.m. is therefore the most productive time to deal with mundane chores like paperwork.

DUMP IT

Don't put junk mail in a pile ready to get rid of later. Open your mail by the wastebin/recycling box and if it's irrelevant, dump it now. Do the same with newspapers. Once you've read them, put them in the recycling box at once, not when they've grown into a 3- foot pile by the television

DELEGATE IT

Do you really need to action this piece of paper yourself or can someone else do it? Use your resources. "The amount of high-level managers I

According to the Buffalo Organization for Social and Technological Innovation, you can increase productivity by 15 per cent simply by having a well-designed office. You're also less likely to end up with backpain, headaches and fatigue – and you could even reduce stress

SEATING
A Royal Navy study found that uncomfortable seating decreased the amount of work officers achieved. The perfect chair should be adjustable in height. But it should also have a movable seat and back rest so you can adopt the perfect position. The chair should be high enough for your keyboard to be at elbow height so your wrists can be flat as you type. Your feet should be flat on the floor – or rested on a footstool or even a phonebook. You should tilt the back of the chair very slightly forward. The seat of the chair should not press against the back of your knees. Armrests should be removed

LIGHT
Fit flicker-free lights to avoid stress and headaches. Ensure that light does not glare on the computer screen – by reducing this in one office, ergonomics firm ErgoWeb.inc decreased feelings of fatigue by 50 per cent

TEMPERATURE
The perfect working temperature is 65–70 degrees Fahrenheit

AIR
Air-conditioning, computers and central heating all lead to dry and poor-quality air that can mess with skin and lead to increased risk of infection. A glass of water on your desk can help increase humidity and certain plants will help reduce radiowaves emitted from your computer. Spider plants or Chinese evergreens work best

NOISE
Recent studies have proved that those open-plan offices companies seem to like so much are unproductive as people find the noise level hard to deal with. While you can often tune out a certain level of noise, excessive or distracting noise (like colleagues talking about deals you want to be in on, or projects you know nothing about) will decrease the amount you get done

COLOUR
Depending on your business you may want to alter your décor. Peach, beige and pale pink stimulate creativity so are good for writers, designers and ideas people. Blue, turquoise or green help you concentrate and so work for accountants, clerks, etc. Bright red makes you nervous and is probably best avoided

meet who write mundane letters is ridiculous," says Allison Van Norman. If you're a complete control freak, bear in mind that we talk quicker than the average typist types. Dictating what you want to say to be transcribed is quicker than typing it yourself.

Clearing the Backlog

The chances are that you can visualize the big pile of paper on your desk that hasn't yet met the superefficient new you. Okay, tomorrow go into work or wherever that paper lies an hour early (this is much better than staying late when you're more likely to try and finish a task instead). When you get there, put the paperwork in the middle of your desk and go through each piece in turn. "As you do so, ask yourself one of these three questions," says Allison Van Norman:

1 **"Do I need this piece of paper?" What's the worst thing that could happen if you threw it away? If it's nothing, dump it. If you need it, determine why and therefore where it should go. If it needs acting on, do it now or put it in your "to do" file (remember you've booked an appointment here). If it needs filing, then file it.**

2 **"Is it on file somewhere else (or should it be)?" If you know there's a copy elsewhere then lose it. If you're saving it for an address, phone number or fact, note these in the relevant address book or notepad and throw away the paper.**

3 **"Does it actually belong in my files?" Sentimental things don't belong here – they belong in your nostalgia box at home. Take them there.**

Be ruthless – 80 per cent of the things people file never get looked at again.

Summary

Most of the space in our homes is filled with clutter that we never use

Dejunking clutter frees up space, money and time, and many experts believe it can also clear your mind and body

Often we clutter out of habit or tradition – even your gender can make a difference

Most of us have inefficient storage, not insufficient storage

We handle 300 pieces of paper a day and spend a week a year looking for things we've lost

A dejunked office space will increase the amount you get done and reduce problems such as backache and fatigue

Action Plan

Decide where your clutter is causing the most problems and/or work out how much it's costing you

Follow the D.E.J.U.N.K. rules to clear everything out. Send off everything that needs mending; throw away everything that has to go; take all the good items to charity shops or car boot sales

Reassess your space to ensure you're using everything to its best advantage

Continually reassess – is everything still in its right place? Is there a better place?

After a year, head up to the loft and throw away everything in those boxes

Spend one day clearing your desk and setting up a maintenance system

Try to reduce the paper you receive

Assess your office space

Chapter 2
Dejunk Your Image

UP UNTIL A FEW MONTHS AGO, I estimate I wasted about three hours a week, with my head in a box in the corner of my bedroom, trying to find clean gym kit. The problem was, all my clothes are black, the box is black and it was in a pretty dark corner – the more I churned around in the endless T-shirts, the more messed up it got. Every day I'd start tidying it but get fed up as soon as I found the thing I was looking for and throw it all back in. I spent hours hunting through stuff I never wore to get to the stuff I wore daily. Now, the box has gone. There are shelves in my wardrobe for gym kit – all the other stuff that was in the box is either folded up on other shelves or (more likely) in the bin. I now take five minutes to find my gym kit – and I go to the gym more often because it's less hassle to get there. I'm less stressed first thing in the morning (the time medical experts agree is the most dangerous to get het up), I'm healthier because I'm working out more often, and I've made a fortune selling off all the stuff I no longer wear. From clearing out one box, I've saved time, made money, decreased stress and got fitter – and what works for me will work for anyone else.

So now you can see why we're getting into this right at the beginning of the dejunk plan. We may see our clothes merely as something we wear, but on average we spend 50 minutes a day getting up and out of the house. According to Kim Johnson Gross from the bible of pared-down dressing, Chic Simple, dejunking your closet cuts this down to ten minutes. "Making that initial investment of time is worth it. If you simplify the mundane parts of your life, you have the time to find those moments of joy that you're usually too busy to appreciate," she explains.

The truth is that most of us have far more clothes than we will ever wear and twice as many as we did in the 1960s, say house-builders Wimpey. For example, the average woman owns 20 to 30 pairs of shoes, the average man has a dozen – both sexes generally wear just two. We wear 20 per cent of our clothes 80 per cent of the time; the rest of the stuff just sits there waiting for black-tie dos, for us to lose enough weight to get into them or to paint the bathroom/weed the garden. Yet we still put more and more into the wardrobe – and most of the things we buy are not necessary.

The cluttered space behind the closet door is also governed by how much we paid for things. "I once bought a £300 black linen suit in a sale," explains Jane, an advertising manager. "It looked gorgeous on me and I wore it to work one day when I had a major presentation and a dinner to go to. By 11.30 it looked as if I had slept in it. It was so creased that when I stood up to do my presentation I was mortified and fluffed the whole thing. I have never worn it again and it just hangs in my wardrobe. Every time I look it I remember that I lost the contract but every time I go to throw it away I just think how much I paid for it and I can't do it." If anything else in Jane's life was bringing her that much misery it'd be gone, but a little price label is stopping her chucking it. No matter how much you paid for something, it's not worth keeping if you don't wear it. While it's nice to have an Armani suit or whatever your particular item is, if it doesn't fit and you're schlepping around all day in a pair of Gap chinos, it's a waste of space. Not to mention a drain on your emotions as you start thinking, "If only I still looked as good as I did when I used to wear that."

From now on, the first rule of fashion in your wardrobe shouldn't have anything to do with length, colour or style. It should be to remember that you're judged by the clothes that you wear, not the ones that are hanging in your closet – if your best clothes are behind closed doors, what good are they doing you?

The Once-and-for-all Closet Clear Plan

Most of us don't wear things for four reasons:

- **We haven't got anything to go with them**
- **They don't fit/suit us**
- **We can't find them**
- **We think they're too expensive for day-to-day wear**

By following the dejunk plan, all these problems will come to an end. It will probably take a while (especially for women who, professional organizers say, find it extremely hard to part with clothing), so set aside a day or at least half a day. Now go to your wardrobe, your drawers, the box under the bed – everywhere you store clothes. Pull everything out – yes, that's right, everything. It may look like Armageddon, but it is only when you get every piece of clothing together that you will realize that you have twenty white shirts (and only ever wear three) and seventeen pairs of shoes.

STEP ONE — CLEAR OUT

Pile it all on the bed or the floor and then start to weed things out. Just as when you were clearing clutter from your home, you should spend no more than five seconds on each item. First, you need to weed out everything that's completely useless or superfluous to your needs. This will vary depending on your wardrobe but generally things that fit into any of the following categories should go either in the bin or to the charity shop.

- **Anything that doesn't fit you – or that doesn't flatter you**
- **Anything you've owned for more than two months that still has the price tag on**
- **Any fashion items you're waiting to come back in**
- **Anything with a stain that won't come out, a rip-off that's faded, threadbare or generally tatty**
- **Anything that looks like you'd wear it to a costume party**
- **Any more than one outfit that you think you'll wear to clean the windows, paint the house, do the gardening – unless you're a window cleaner, painter or gardener**
- **Anything you would be ashamed to be seen in by other people**

Everything else left should either be clothes you wear all the time or items you'd completely forgotten about but that you would like to wear all the time.

STEP TWO — AUDIT

The next stage of the closet clear is to determine whether the pieces you've got left work together and the key to doing this is the wardrobe graph.

On a piece of paper, draw a graph. Things you wear on the bottom go down the side; things you wear on top run along the top. Tick what goes with what – in terms of everyday items, everything you keep should go with at least three different items. As for occasion outfits, everything should be able to take you through at least two sorts of occasion (a wedding and an evening do, for example).

If there are items that don't fit the bill, ask what would it take to make this item work. If the answer is nothing, if the item doesn't work and will never work, it has to go. If, however, you believe the answer is something simple like a white T-shirt, and that item will go with at least two other things, keep the item and invest in the new thing (you'll get at least three outfits that way). Just make sure you follow the replace rules in Step Three.

Do You Really Want to Keep That?

Some items in your wardrobe may not be saying all that you want them to say. Studies have revealed that people react more favourably towards people they find attractive – and people who dress well are deemed to be more attractive (and more sucessful) than those who are dressed in a scruffy fashion. Juries are influenced by it, voters are influenced by it – and personnel officers are influenced by it. A study by the Center for Creative Leadership in the US discovered 35 per cent of women who were denied promotion to executive level were told that their poor image was to blame. How you look sends many messages to the outside world. While you dejunk your image, bear in mind what the following say about you:

JUMPERS: A study from the University of Minnesota discovered that thin and supple knits say you're sophisticated and mature; deep V-necks make you appear romantic and sensual; and medium-weight knits say you're both logical and efficient

LAYERABLE CLOTHING: According to author Toby Fischer Mirkin in her book *Dress Code*, you're seen as more authoritative if you wear layers

SHORT SKIRTS: Australian research reveals that people think women in short skirts are open-minded and creative, and women in long slim skirts are sophisticated and intellectual

GREY CLOTHING: Fischer Mirkin also reveals that grey is seen as a colour of refinement, class and efficiency. You give off strong messages of power and economic and social mobility if you wear grey. If you want someone to spend more time with you, keep clothes in warm colours (reds, terracotta, etc.). Studies reveal that time spent with someone wearing a suit in a warm colour seems to go faster than time spent with someone wearing cooler colours

DETAILS: "If you want to impress men, keep your best shoes; if you want to impress women, concentrate on details like cut and fit," says image consultant Mary Spillane from Colour Me Beautiful

HAIR COLOUR: Research from the University of Coventry shows that hair stereotypes do exist. Platinum blondes are voted less intelligent, brunettes are seen as shy and natural blondes are popular

STEP THREE – REPLACE

The final step in a closet clear plan that really will last for ever is to look carefully at what you buy in the future. Just as the clothes that work for you probably follow a pattern, so will those that you just got rid of. Look carefully at what you threw out. Were they...

THINGS THAT DIDN'T FIT: Ask yourself why this is. "Many people who've lost weight find it hard to buy clothes in the right size because they still have this image in their head of the person they once were," says image consultant Barney Tremblay. "The same happens to people who are unhappy with their body, they buy things for the size they want to be, convincing themselves that by doing this they'll lose the weight. A new dress doesn't make you lose weight – no matter how expensive it is – only the right mindset will do that."

THINGS THAT DIDN'T SUIT YOU: Why do you do this? If it's because you're not sure what looks good on you, the next time you go shopping you should look at three things:

PROPORTION: Make sure things are the right length for your body and the other items you plan to wear it with. If the proportions wrong, the outfit's wrong.

FIT: Check the sleeves are the right length and that a jacket doesn't bulge at the seams and ensure that the cut of the outfit fits the shape of your figure. Straight up and down outfits suit straight up and down people, curvy figures should go for tailored styles.

COLOUR: Outfits should suit your skintone and the other colours in your wardrobe. Barney Tremblay recommends you wear 60 per cent of one colour and 40 per cent of another.

THINGS THAT DIDN'T GO WITH ANYTHING ELSE: Chances are these were impulse buys or panic buys for occasions like weddings or job interviews. Try to avoid this by thinking through what you're buying and ensuring that every item goes with at least two other items in your wardrobe.

DO YOU BUY THINGS THAT FALL APART? When money's tight it is hard to justify spending a lot on clothes, but often it is better to spend extra on something of good quality to ensure it lasts. "The key to determining if this is worth doing is the cost per wear ratio," says stylist Jane Nicholson. "Look at how much something costs and think how many times you'll wear it. Does it now seem like value for money? A £200 jacket you can wear four times a month for the next two years is better value than a £50 one that'll fall to pieces in three months. The rule of the CPW ratio is spend more on items you'll wear often, skimp on those for occasional wear."

THE PERFECT WHITE SHIRT

According to fashion buyer Michael Duffy, the perfect white shirt is made from 50 per cent cotton, 50 per cent polyester. "It's known as easycare/easy wear fabric," he explains. "The cotton makes the shirt comfortable, but the polyester ensures that you don't have to spend hours ironing the garment. Only buy shirts with plain white buttons and small collars, as these will not date."

THE PERFECT BUSINESS SUIT

It may not sound glamorous, but the perfect business suit is made from 97 per cent polyester and 3 per cent Lycra. "Wool may be lovely to wear but within a few hours you'll have creases around the elbows and the backs of the knees, which don't look professional," explains Michael Duffy. "In terms of colour, polyester works best in shades of navy, black or grey. When you try the jacket on, check the fit across the back, under the arms and with the jacket done up. A general rule is that if the lining of the jacket is well finished, the jacket itself will be well made – if a company is going to skimp on anything, it will be lining."

THE PERFECT PAIR OF SHOES

Cordwainers College recommends that to find a pair of shoes that'll last and don't pinch, you should do the following tests:

1 Hold the backs together and check they are of equal height, then put each shoe down to make sure they sit flat

2 Can you slip a pencil under the shoe's toe? If not, it won't rock as you walk

3 If you can pull the insole or innersock away, then they haven't used the right adhesive and it'll ruck up

4 Run your finger around the inner sock. You shouldn't feel any bumps from nails. Check for bad stitching inside

5 Choose leather, it's best for comfort

THE PERFECT PAIR OF TRAINERS

Personal trainer Robin Drummond explains what to look for in running shoes: "A good training shoe should be cut low at the back and be soft around the Achilles tendon. Nike are narrow and Reebok are wider. Good trainers should have about 1cm space between your big toe and the end. Your toes should be free to move and the top of your foot shouldn't be crushed by the laces. Before putting them on, run your finger around the inside – rough stitching will chafe."

THE PERFECT BRA

According to Fenwick of Bond Street, to buy a perfect bra you should first get measured. In order to give proper support, the bra should fit snugly around the ribcage and under the bust. The strap should not ride up. The colour depends on the bra's function. If you want to wear it under a T-shirt, it should be "nude". A good tip – the bigger your bust, the higher the Lycra content needed

DO YOU BUY THINGS FOR FASHION? This is fine, but perhaps you should think about using the CPW ratio for fashion items so at least when you have to throw them out in a year you won't feel cheated. And you will throw them out – there's no point in waiting for things to come back into fashion. Bellbottoms took twenty years and lasted one summer!

Timesaver Tip: The forty-minute clothes shop

Shopping for clothing can take hours. You have to find the style that suits you, find the fit that's right for you and then determine if what you're buying is actually worth the cash. However, Jane Nicholson admits you can cut the time you spend clothes shopping right down.

- **Learn to scan**: *"You can only do a forty-minute shop if you know what you want to buy – be it trousers, a suit or a shirt. Know what it is and head to that department and that department only. Nothing else matters. When you get there, scan – if you want black, only look for black. If you want double-breasted, only look for double-breasted. I can walk in to a store and know within one minute if I'm going to find what I need."*

- **Know your price range**: *"We all have a set pricing strategy for how much we're willing to pay for something – or can afford to pay for it. On a forty-minute shop, only go into the shops that fit your price range."*

- **Know the specialities**: *There's no point going to TopShop or TopMan for a sophisticated black-tie outfit. Different stores are particularly good for different occasions and if time is of the essence you want to choose the widest range. I'd recommend Jigsaw, French Connection and M&S for suiting (both men and women); Gap, for casualwear, M&S for underwear.*

- **Know the sizes**: *"Once you've chosen an item there's nothing more frustrating than getting it to the changing room and discovering it's the wrong size. Different stores cut to different patterns. For women: generally European stores cut small (think Agnès B, Joseph and Kookai) as do those aiming at a younger market (Top Shop); M&S, Next and Miss Selfridge tend to cut pretty standard; Dorothy Perkins, Warehouse and Gap cut large."*

- **Know your quality**: *With a little knowledge, you can spot the perfect buy almost before you put it on, thus preventing the shopping nightmare of finally choosing an item, getting it home and discovering it creases within ten minutes of wearing, or that the shoes you bought rub your feet.*

The Perfect Clothing Plan

A perfectly stored wardrobe increases the speed with which you get out of the house in the morning. So what are the tricks of the trade?

ALLOCATE SPACE: "If you're sharing wardrobe space with a partner, bear in mind women tend to have more long clothing than men," says Barney Tremblay, image consultant. Women generally need more horizontal closet space than men. Typically, in shared closets women need two-thirds of the space, men can make do with one-third.

SHELVE DEAD AREAS: Many items in your wardrobe should be folded rather than hung and this maximizes the space. "Knits should always be folded, as should T-shirts and other casual items. As a general rule, anything that has sharp edges or creases (trousers or pleated skirts) should be hung, as should anything that needs the shape of a hanger to keep its structure, such as a jacket. Other items should be folded," says Tremblay.

USE BOXES OR FOLDAWAY STORAGE: Your storage needs should be able to adapt to changes in your wardrobe. You're not wearing the same types of clothes as you did five or ten years ago – why would you need to store them in the same way?

NEVER HANG THINGS IN OUTFITS: "You'll get more wear from things in your wardrobe if you hang items separately," says Barney Tremblay. "It helps you be more creative."

HAVE A POCKET HOLDER: Unlike women, who carry everything in their handbags, men tend to put keys and cash in their pockets and can waste time trying to find things left in old pockets. As a rule, when you hang your jacket up every night, you should empty all the pockets into this drawer/bowl, so you'll always know where items are the next day.

DON'T USE WIRE HANGERS: Not only are they bad for your clothes, they also have a tendency to tangle, which makes hanging clothes more of a chore than it needs to be.

HANG BY SEASON: It's a lot easier to organize your wardrobe if it's arranged by season.

SHOE CUBBIES: Keep each pair together and increase the number of pairs of shoes you can keep dramatically. In an average cupboard, on a 1 ft square floor space, you can keep three pairs of shoes without shoe cubbies, whereas with shoe cubbies you could keep about eighteen pairs.

LAUNDRY BASKETS: In a busy house you should have more than one laundry basket so you can sort washes by colour and just carry the whole bag to the machine.

Dejunking Your Bathroom

The world-wide toiletries market was worth around £4.3billion in 1997. Women are the biggest culprits in this area, but men are catching up.

SO HOW MUCH OF THIS STUFF DO WE REALLY NEED?

Not much. According to dermatologist Professor Ronald Marks, all our skin actually needs is sunscreen and a basic moisturizer. "Any oil and water blend will do for both men and women," he explains. As for hair, all the average head needs is a shampoo and conditioner, according to London hairdresser Daniel Hersheson, "but it must be right for you." Make-up is another huge growth industry. "Women own far more make-up than they need and will ever wear," says make-up artist Virginia Nichols. "All you really need is a foundation (or, if you have good skin, a concealer), mascara and two lipsticks – one for day and one for night. Blondes can get by with a pinky brown and an orangey red, brunettes with pink and true red, redheads with a gingery brown and an orangey red and girls with darker skins should choose a brick red and a plum."

AND HOW LONG SHOULD WE HANG ON TO IT?

The other thing that leads to cluttered bathroom shelves is the fact that we don't throw things away fast enough. Here's our guide to what needs chucking out when.

VITAMIN PILLS: Last three to five years but are very susceptible to moisture.

MOUTHWASH: Lasts for up to three years – if you don't drink out of the bottle.

MEDICINES: Should be marked with an expiry date and should be dumped on it – or before if you get the tablets damp, or they have started to disintegrate. If you've lost the pack, bin anything more than six months old, just in case.

SHAMPOO AND CONDITIONER: Should last for up to three years.

CONDOMS: Last for up to five years if stored carefully – i.e. in a cool, dark place.

DEODORANT: Lasts about two and a half years.

CONTACT LENS SOLUTION: Manufacturers say it lasts twenty-eight days. In reality, if you've kept the bottle clean and the lid on, it'll keep for six months.

HAIR REMOVAL CREAM: Stops working after about two years.

MAKE-UP: All cosmetics must last 30 months.

SUNSCREEN: Unopened, it'll last 30 months. Should be replaced after every trip.

PERFUME: Once opened, it will last six months.

Timesaver Tip: The five-minute make-over

Make-up artist Virginia Nichols explains how to look groomed when you're running late:

Apply tinted moisturizer – it blends faster than foundation

Apply all-in-one eyeshadow and blusher to the cheeks, eye sockets and temples

Apply mascara

Fill in the lips with lip pencil – stick to a neutral shade so you don't make mistakes

Brush your eyebrows – you'll be amazed how it finishes off your face, eliminating the need for precise blending

Summary

We wear 20 per cent of our clothes 80 per cent of the time

Dejunking your closet could save you ten days' worth of getting-ready time a year

You can buy cheaper clothes without anyone noticing, if you follow the budget rules

Knowing where and how to shop can cut clothes-shopping time in half

Storing clothes correctly increases their lifespan and decreases your getting-ready time

We buy far more toiletries than our body actually needs to stay healthy

This leads to us keeping them too long, which decreases their efficiency

Action Plan

Go through your wardrobe and throw out anything that doesn't fit; that you've never worn; that's damaged; or that looks ridiculous

Do the wardrobe graph to determine what you need

Replace, following the replace rules

Assess your clothes storage

Throw away anything out of date in the bathroom – and look at what you really need in your life

Chapter 3
Dejunk Your Body

How Your Body Affects Your Life

When someone asks you how you are feeling, how often do you answer "excellent"? For most of us, not often. More commonly you'll respond with an answer like "tired", "stressed" or that all-encompassing meaningless remark, "I'm fine". But all these responses are not fine. A healthy, dejunked body should not be tired all the time, it shouldn't need three cups of coffee before it will function normally in the morning, and it shouldn't be surviving on a knife-edge of stress – yet many see these things as normal. The chances are, you bought this book because you're not happy about something – be it the amount of time you have, the amount of money you don't have or the emotions you'd like to have. Well, looking after your body is one part of solving these problems. "If you asked a biologist, a chemist and a physiologist to say where the brain stops and the body begins, they couldn't do it," says nutritionist Patrick Holford. Every part of your life interacts – and what you put into your body controls what you get out of it.

The problem is that the body was not designed for everything we throw at it. It was not designed for refined food, caffeine-filled drinks and polluted air. It was not designed to live in a country such as the UK, where every year we ingest a million tons of food chemicals, 200 million alcoholic drinks and 83 billion cigarettes, where every year the average person breathes in 2 grammes of solid pollution, eats 12 lb of food additives and ingests up to a gallon of pesticides. What this means is that, instead of spending its time functioning normally, concentrating on processing the maximum number of nutrients from food and ensuring that cell repair and immunity are functioning at full capacity, the body is too busy dealing with all the junk that we throw at it. This leads to lethargy, skin problems like spots or cellulite and decreased immunity. It also increases congestion in the system. Mucous membranes clog up, leading to sneezing or asthma-type symptoms, the skin can look grey and dull and it's estimated the average US or European colon carries within it over 5 lb of half-digested red meat plus another 5–10 lb of impacted toxic waste. And we haven't even discussed the effects on energy and mood.

So What Difference Does Dejunking Your Body Make?

Ninety-eight per cent of your body is constructed from the substances that entered it during the last twelve months – including all the pollutants, pesticides and other junk you took in. To function properly, we need a mix of 59 nutrients daily and if you're missing even one of these, problems occur. Take vitamin B12: you need just 2 microgrammes of this daily (about the size of a speck of dust), but if you don't get that, your health may be seriously affected. Eating well is one of the most important things you can do to dejunk your life. If you haven't got a healthy body, the other elements don't really matter.

So How Much of YOUR Body Needs to Be Dejunked?

According to Derbyshire-based nutritionist Esther Mills, very few people have a toxin-free body, but you can get one. "It would take an extremely nutritious diet for at least a year to clean the average system," she explains. However, some of us have more need for a body overhaul than others. To find out what kind of shape you're in, do the quiz Esther has devised, below. For each section, tick the answers that apply to you. Then, at the end of section, add up your totals. The total of all three sections adds up to your dejunk factor – the higher the score, the more you need to dejunk and the more areas of your life you'll free up by doing so.

(Tick all those questions to which you would answer yes.)

WHAT ARE YOU EATING?
>   Do you eat red meat more than three times a week?
>   Do you eat full-fat dairy products?
>   Do you prefer white bread, pasta and rice to wholemeal versions?
>   Do you eat ready meals or processed foods more than three times a week?
>   Do you eat less than three pieces of fruit a day?
>   Do you eat less than three servings of vegetables a day?
>   **TOTAL:**

DO YOU HAVE HARMFUL HABITS?
>   Do you add salt to your food?
>   Do you add sugar to tea or coffee?
>   Do you drink more than one cup of coffee a day?
>   Do you smoke?
>   Do you drink more than one alcoholic drink daily?
>   **TOTAL:**

DO YOU LIVE IN A TOXIC ENVIRONMENT?
>   Do you work on a computer?
>   Do you live or work on a main road?

Do you drive to work?

Are the windows of your home open for an hour or less daily?

Do you have a mobile phone?

Do you work in an air-conditioned office?

TOTAL:

DO YOU HAVE ANY TOXIC SYMPTOMS?

(Tick any you suffer from regularly.)

Fatigue

Headaches

Sinus or nasal problems

Muscle and joint pains

Insomnia

Skin problems

Stress

Allergies

Cellulite

TOTAL:

How to Dejunk Your Body

The best way to dejunk your body is to change your diet. Adopting an eating regime that maximizes nutrients and decreases your intake of high-fat, high-sugar foods will help prevent any further damage hitting your system. In order to give yourself the best possible advantage, you should also try a short detoxification programme first.

The best way to do this is to restrict the amount and range of foods you eat for a period of time. "Detoxing can take many forms, from the extreme of a complete fast to merely removing congestive elements in your diet," says Elson M. Haas, physician and author of *The Detox Diet*. "But whatever methods you use I believe detoxing is the missing link in Western medicine and if we used it more in our daily lives we could heal and prevent a great deal of illness."

The extent to which you detox is obviously up to you and the results you want to get. Obviously, the longer you do it for, the better the results will be. However, a longer plan can be difficult to fit into many lifestyles, as there are side-effects. You could get headaches, bad breath and fatigue – in an ideal world, you should schedule the first few days of a dejunk for a quiet long weekend and spend the time in bed. If you do choose the longer plan, make sure it's not a frantic week at work – or one with lots of socializing.

Peter is a lawyer who was suffering from extreme stress and energy swings. It would get to the middle of the afternoon and he'd lose all motivation, which would just increase his stress levels. Most of his meals were taken in the office and as such his diet was high in fat, sugar and refined carbohydrates which were actually causing his problems. Peter went on a plan devised by nutritionist Patrick Holford. It cut all stimulants like coffee and sugar from his diet, it also swapped refined carbohydrates for wholemeal varieties and decreased fat and prescribed a daily multivitamin, extra vitamin C and a dose of chromium piclonate (which helps level out blood sugar). After a few weeks, Peter had noticed an incredible difference. "It's like I'm on a natural high now, not a sugar buzz. I have level energy throughout the day and the fact that I'm able to work consistently means I get more done and suffer less stress. I also believe I'm experiencing less reaction to stress generally. I don't feel like I'm always rushing from A to B."

Sandra believes changing her diet actually saved her marriage. "I was a junk food addict," she explained. "And as such I was experiencing dreadful mood swings. If I was hungry I'd snap at my husband and my ability to deal with stress was practically non-existent. My partner is normally extremely placid but when he went through a period of job stress my sniping got on top of him and we were arguing all the time. My daughter explained that too much sugar can affect insulin levels in the body and lead to mood swings, so I cut out all my sugary foods and white carbohydrates. I ate more brown rice, increased my protein levels and lowered fat. The difference was practically instantaneous. I stopped snapping, had more energy and actually gained about three hours a day where I no longer had to flop into bed the minute I'd finished dinner. I actually managed to sit and sort out my husband's accounts, which decreased his stress levels. I do think it prevented us needing counselling."

The One-day Dejunk

This is easy. Pick a fruit and for one day eat just that fruit and drink bottled water. Any fruit (except bananas) is allowed – but the more water the fruit you choose contains, the better. Watermelon and grapes give best results, or if you're worried about hunger, try apples. They contain high levels of pectin, which has been shown to decrease hunger. Expect to eat six or seven mini fruit meals that day and keep drinking water. You can also drink herbal teas, but avoid tea or coffee as they contain caffeine. You should also try not to smoke and, if you get a headache, don't take a painkiller, as they can destroy nutrients.

The Weekend Dejunk

DAY ONE
As above

DAY TWO

BREAKFAST: Continue with fruit

LUNCH: Serve a mixed salad of whatever vegetables you like – so long as they are raw: try a mix of lettuce, cucumber, cherry tomatoes, carrots, red cabbage, beansprouts and mange tout

EVENING MEAL: Steam or lightly stir-fry another selection of vegetables with a little fresh ginger (this is a great system purifier) and serve with 2 oz (raw weight) brown rice

Drink at least two litres of water throughout the day. If you get hungry, snack on watery fruits or raw vegetables. If you want a hot drink, try herbal teas which contain no caffeine.

The One-week Plan

Every day, begin your diet with a glass of warm water (not from the hot tap – water from the hot tap is kept in tanks, which can increase levels of bacteria; instead, boil water and let it cool) with a little lemon juice. Because there's a two-day fruit fast on this regime it's probably best that you begin with day one on a Friday: days two and three will therefore fall on a weekend.

DAY ONE

Pre-prepare day. Week-long detoxes can be a bit of a shock to the system so on the first day wean yourself off nasties like coffee, tea and other caffeinated beverages; refined carbohydrates like white bread, pasta, rice etc.; sugar and meat.

DAYS TWO AND THREE

Fruit days: as per the one-day dejunk, eat one type of fruit a day. You can choose the same fruit for two days or switch between days. Drink at least two litres of water – more if you can. Again, herbal teas are allowed.

DAYS FOUR AND FIVE

This reintroduces a variety of foods into your diet but concentrates mainly on raw foods that are digested easily by your body and increase your nutrient intake.

BREAKFAST: Fruit

LUNCH: Mixed salad – you can make this as big as you like and it can contain as many different types of vegetable as you like; the only rules are that they are all raw and that you include at least two water-based vegetables like cucumber, lettuce, beansprouts, celery and tomato

EVENING MEAL: Stir-fry another selection of vegetables with a little olive oil and ginger. Do not cook the veg for more than two minutes: you want them warm, not soggy! If you are hungry, you can also add 2 oz brown rice

DAYS SIX AND SEVEN

These ease you back into cooked food and allow the use of protein and fat. They're in-between days, but you should include at least two days like this in your weekly diet every week.

BREAKFAST: Fruit – mix up a selection of fruits, or if you're sick of raw fruit by now, whisk up a smoothie with a little orange juice or skimmed milk

LUNCH: Salad or stir-fry (no rice this time, I'm afraid) as before

EVENING MEAL: 4 oz of chicken or white fish, grilled or poached. Selection of steamed vegetables or salad, 2 oz brown rice

After a fast like this, your system should be cleansed and you should be feeling more energized. But don't just go back to a junk-food eating plan and undo all your good work. Instead, follow the dejunk diet plan.

The Dejunk Diet for Life

This is not a day-to-day eating plan that'll result in you trying to buy mung beans in the local QuickieMart. That approach is pointless. One diet does not fit all in terms of health or weight-loss. As a 9½-stone woman who sits typing all day, my nutrient intake is going to be completely different from (and irrelevant to) that of a 14-stone builder. "Diets have to be tailored to the individual," explains nutritionist Anita Bean. There are, however, some rules you should abide by and ways to work out the *likely* levels that are going to ensure optimum results for you, and from these come the healthy eating plan that follows. It's not a weight-loss plan – the idea of this diet is to increase your nutrients and decrease your toxins in a way that'll ensure your body and your brain are working to maximum advantage. If you want to read a diet for weight loss, I'd recommend *The 30-Day FatBurner Diet* by Patrick Holford. It's sane, scientific and successful – and there aren't that many weight-loss plans out there that can say that. This is also not a plan for marathon runners or serious athletes: you need a lot more food than is mentioned here and your best read is *The Complete Guide to Sports Nutrition* by Anita Bean. The diet that follows is the diet for Mr and Mrs Average. Just one thing before you read on, get a pen, paper and a calculator. No one said a healthy body wouldn't involve maths.

PROTEIN

Protein builds our body up. Without it, you lose muscle mass, damaged tissues wouldn't be repaired and your hormones would be way out of kilter.

HOW MUCH DO YOU NEED?

According to the Department of Health, the average sedentary man or woman needs 0.75 g per kilogramme of weight of protein a day. Therefore, my 9½-stone (60 kg) frame needs about 45 g, my 14-stone builder friend needs 66 g.

HOW TO GET IT

Meat, fish, dairy products and protein-based legumes and grains are the main sources – just watch out for fat content. Animal-based sources of protein can be high in saturated fat, which does not make up a big part of the dejunk diet.

TEN TOP SOURCES OF PROTEIN

Chicken (6 oz portion gives 38 g protein)
White and oily fish (6 oz portion gives 30 g protein)
Tinned tuna (4 oz = 25 g)
Red meat (4 oz = 32 g)
Skimmed or semi-skimmed milk (½ pint = 10 g)

Cottage cheese (4 oz=15 g)
Yoghurt (1 carton=8 g)
Baked beans ($^1/_2$ tin=10 g
Lentils (8 oz boiled=15 g)
Tofu (4 oz=9 g)

CARBOHYDRATES

Carbohydrates are the main source of fuel for our body. They should also make up the mainstay of our diet. A diet low in carbs is likely to lead to fatigue and possibly even increased stress levels, as carbs are calming foods. If you're an insomniac, increasing the levels of carbs in your diet may also help you sleep, as it stimulates the hormones that promote sleep.

HOW MUCH DO WE NEED?

4–5 g per kilogramme of body weight a day.

HOW TO GET THEM

Carbs come in two types: unrefined carbs (like wholewheat bread, brown rice, etc.) which supply long, lasting energy; and refined carbs like white bread or sugary foods which create energy rushes – followed by drops in energy. The dejunk diet is based around unrefined carbs.

SEVEN TOP SOURCES OF CARBOHYDRATES

Wholemeal bread (1 slice=16 g)
Baked potato (160 g=29 g)
Bananas (one=19 g)
Pasta (75 g=56 g)

How Dejunking Your Diet Can Dejunk Your Life

YOU'LL BE SMARTER: Studies at the Massachusetts Institute of Technology revealed that people who ate a lot of refined sugars had lower IQs than those who ate refined carbohydrates. People who used vitamin C supplements had higher IQ scores than non-supplementers

YOU'LL GET SICK LESS OFTEN: Research has shown those with high intakes of vitamin C have 34 per cent fewer sick days than others

YOU'LL THINK MORE CLEARLY: "Physical detox helps mental detox," says Elson M. Hass. "Many people experience new levels of clarity after detoxing their diet. When our body has eliminated its toxic build-up we feel lighter and able to experience the moment and the future."

PEOPLE WILL LIKE YOU MORE: Study subjects react more favourably to someone they believe eats a healthy diet than someone they're told eats a diet high in doughnuts and ice-cream. Studies at Arizona State University found people believe them to be more friendly, more energetic and more ambitious than the non-healthy eater

YOU'RE MORE LIKELY TO GET WHAT YOU WANT FROM RELATIONSHIPS: Elson M. Haas believes that dejunking your diet can help you deal better with relationships and stabilize emotions. "Detoxing the body helps us re-evaluate our lives, to make changes, or to clear abuses. Many people start or end relationships after a period of detoxing."

Rice (50 g=43 g)
Baked beans (135 g=20 g)
Sweetcorn (125 g=25 g)

FAT

There is no recommended per-body-weight calculation for fat. Instead it's expressed as a percentage of the total calories you should eat in a day. How many calories you need in a day is determined by your basal metabolic rate. This is the amount of calories you burn every day just by breathing, pumping blood, etc. To work this out you multiply your weight in kilogrammes by 0.9 and then multiply this by 24. On top of this, you need to add some calories actually to get up and go places. Mr and Mrs Average who don't exercise should now multiply this figure by 1.3. If you work out a couple of times a week, multiply it by 1.5. That gives you the total number of calories that you should absorb in one day to maintain your weight – fat calories should make up 25 per cent of these.

To work out how many grammes of fat this means you can eat in a day, take the total number of calories you are supposed to eat in a day, multiply it by 25 per cent, then divide it by 9 (this is the amount of calories in one gram of fat). This is how many fat grammes you should eat in a day. Just one final thing before you see what goodies you can consume – no more than 10 per cent of your calories should come from saturated fat, so read those labels carefully.

HOW TO GET IT

Most of the fat in your diet will come from other sources like protein – there's no need to ladle 15 fat grammes worth of butter on to your toast every morning. However, if you are choosing fat-based foods, the best are those containing mono-saturated fats.

THE FOUR TOP SOURCES OF FAT

Olive oil
Other oils made from seeds or nuts
Avocados
Nuts

FRUITS AND VEGETABLES

There are no calorie requirements for fruit and vegetables – all you've got to remember is that you should be eating *at least* five portions of fresh fruit and vegetables a day. The more fruit and vegetables you eat, the more nutrients you'll take in and the better your body will respond. Simple, really. Even simpler are the good choices and bad choices – all vegetables and fruit are good, so eat as much of them as you like. However, to superload your nutrients, choose prunes/raisins, berries, plums and oranges, or kale/spinach, brussels sprouts and broccoli. Research from Tufts University in Boston has revealed that these contain the highest levels of cancer-fighting nutrients. If you really want to be healthy you should also eat a majority of those fruits and vegetables raw or at most lightly steamed or stir-fried.

STIMULANTS

A health fanatic would tell you that you shouldn't have any stimulants in your life – no caffeine, no alcohol, no cigarettes, no sugar, no nothing. But I'm not a health fanatic and therefore almost all of the above are allowable in any healthy eating regime to some extent – but before you indulge, you should know the facts.

CAFFEINE

The average person consumes 10 lb of caffeine a year. This is not good. Caffeine increases fatigue (yes, really – it stops you sleeping), irritability and can even cause heart palpitations. In an ideal world we'd consume no more than 500 mg of caffeine a day (the equivalent of about six cups of coffee), but before you head to the Krups machine, just remember that caffeine is everywhere – so it's easy to overload. An aspirin contains 30 mg, 100 g of chocolate contains up to 43 mg and tea can contain up to 80 mg – watch your levels.

ALCOHOL

The odd drink doesn't do much harm, but don't necessarily believe the hype about alcohol being good for you. If you're under 40 and reading this, I'm sorry, I have bad news. According to American health gurus at the Center for Science in the Public Interest, the detrimental health benefits of drinking those two glasses of red wine a day actually outweigh the heart disease protection (if you're over 40, this balance switches, so cheers). Ideally, have no more than one alcoholic drink a day and make it red wine.

CIGARETTES

Sorry, if you want to dejunk your life, you shouldn't smoke. According to research by temp company Office Angels, smokers waste three hours a week taking breaks (and it's becoming increasingly likely that they'll have to work longer hours to make up for it). At 1999 prices, the average smoker spends £1,200 a year on their habit (and that doesn't include matches or lighters) and smoking is always among the list of the three biggest turn-offs in surveys from dating agencies. If you want to quit, seek help. Quitline are a brilliant organization who will advise you on what to do. Call them on 0800 002200.

Timesaver tip: The five-minute healthy meal

If you come in late, it can be a pain, trying to eat healthily. Healthy food often seems to take ages to prepare and it can be easier to put a ready meal in the oven – or pick up a takeaway on the way home. However, we have learnt the secret of a dejunked healthy eating plan. When I approached London's healthy eating bar Gold, they told me the secret to their success was their five-minute red Thai sauce. They use it in wraps (which take just minutes to make) but you could also use it to liven up five-minute stir-fries, put it on some pan-fried fish (guess how long that takes) or I've even just spooned a couple of tbsp over some rice. The sauce itself takes just five minutes' cooking – but then has to be left to cool, so you do have to make it in advance. It keeps in the fridge for a couple of weeks (store it in an airtight container).

RED THAI SAUCE

2 tins of coconut milk

6 fresh chillies

2 leaves of lemongrass

3 bay leaves

3 tbsp of curry paste

salt and pepper to taste

$1/_4$ bunch coriander

1 tbsp of cumin

1 tbsp of paprika

Chop all the fresh herbs finely, mix all the ingredients together and heat so it boils rapidly for 2–3 minutes. Leave to infuse until it has cooled to cold. Place in the fridge and use (hot or cold) as needed.

If you want to try out a wrap, Gold also gave us this recipe:

Stir fry 5 oz of chicken breast cooked in strips. On a half-sheet of Khobez bread (similar to pitta bread) place the chicken, 1–$1^1/_2$ oz of cous cous, 1oz iceberg lettuce and 1–$1^1/_2$ tbsp of red Thai sauce. Roll the bread up and eat like a sandwich.

Timesaver Tip: The two-minute food fatness test

The best way to tell if a food is too fattening is to read the label – it should contain no more than 4 g of fat for every 100 calories of food. If the food doesn't have a label (freshly baked muffins, etc.), an easy way to tell if it contains too much fat is to place it on a paper towel for two minutes. If it leaves a greasy mark, it's too fattening.

Why Exercise is Essential for a Dejunked Life

In a world where we don't have enough time to think, it can be hard to rationalize taking time out to exercise, but that's a false economy. Exercise is one of the single most beneficial ways to enhance every area of your life. The endorphins released in just twenty minutes of hard exercise elevate your mood and energy levels for up to two hours afterwards. Studies show that exercise improves intellectual functions after just one workout. A study in the journal *Medicine and Science in Sports and Exercise* found that physically fit adults scored highest on memory and intelligence; further studies showed it made them more creative. Exercise improves your relationships by helping moderate moods and tensions, plus one US study of 8,000 exercisers found they had a more satisfying sex life than non-exercisers. Exercise could also help you up the career ladder. A recent study found that 78 per cent of people who believe they are successful exercise and get major benefits from it. Only 2 per cent of high-flyers in Birmingham, for example, say they suffered stress – 51 per cent of similarly located couch potatoes say they do feel under pressure. "Exercise teaches you concentration and focus," says personal trainer Sarah Gordon. "Once you finish a workout, you apply this to the rest of your life. Combine this with its benefits in boosting health and longevity and you have a very powerful life enhancer."

However, studies have also shown that most of us know exercise has benefits yet still find it hard to work it into our lives. Sixty per cent of people in a study by the Coors Brewing Company say they would like more time to work out. "Research reveals that when someone is under pressure, their trip to the gym is one of the first things to go," says London-based personal trainer Luke Wilkins. "We don't think of exercise as something that can actually alleviate problems, we just see it as something that adds to our time pressure."

So how can you fit exercise into your life? "The difference is between finding time and making time," says Luke Wilkins. "Many people believe that exercise needs to be a one-off, one-hour commitment two or three times a week, but that's not necessarily true. A recent study from the Cooper Institute of Aerobics Research in Dallas discovered that people who went to the gym for half an hour three to five times a week achieved the same benefits as people who did 30 minutes total 'activity' three to five times a week. This could be done in one go or in ten to fifteen-minute bursts. It seems that it's the total amount of exercise that you do that counts now, not the length of each individual session." Activity has also become the exercise buzzword of the busy life.

Even the Health Education Authority, which once recommended that we all carry

How Exercising Changed My Life

"Exercise has made me realize that nothing is impossible," says Tom, a 32-year-old publishing executive. "I'm 18 stone and I eat, drink and smoke far more than I should. As far as I was concerned, exercise was not something that should be a part of my life. I'd always been the one at school that no one picked for the team and my build was not exactly sprinter material. Then my wife started training for a marathon. She'd never run before, but was getting really into it and nagged me constantly at weekends to go with her. Eventually I gave in. It was a nightmare at first, I thought I was going to die, but eventually I got fitter and I've now run a half marathon. Of course I've got all the normal benefits, I don't get sick as often, I've got more energy and I don't feel as guilty for the drinking and smoking, but there is more to it than that. Exercise was a bugbear. I had always thought I couldn't do it. But then I did – and I ran 13 miles. That gave me so much more confidence. I began to look at other things I had thought were out of my league. I got promotion, I've started scriptwriting and I'm about to go on a scuba course. Mind you, I still run round thinking about what I'm going to eat when I finish."

out twenty minutes of exercise three times a week, has said we should all aim to get twenty to thirty minutes of activity a day. What's the difference? Activity doesn't mean organized planned exercise. It means climbing stairs instead of taking lifts, walking to work or during our lunch breaks, running around the garden with the kids, or taking up a hobby like in-line skating at the weekend. Activity really is the ultimate dejunk exercise; plan to do things that make you happy when you want to do them. You get health and fitness benefits, stress reduction, weight loss, energy boosts – the whole kit and caboodle – and you enjoy it.

However, sometimes we want a more structured exercise plan with established goals, but this is when exercise can go against the dejunk plan. We spend money on gyms or equipment that we then decide we haven't got time to use, we stress because we're not fitting in our allotted exercise time and we get depressed when we quit because it's not working. That's where the following plan can help.

Exercise for a Dejunked Life

The most important element of exercise for a dejunked life is that you choose a plan that you are actually going to stick to. Otherwise any time and/or money that you have spent developing this new habit is going to be wasted. Most people who quit an exercise regime do so within the first three months and studies have revealed that the two main reasons are not seeing the results they were hoping for, and trying to do too much too soon. The point of the dejunked plan is therefore to try and ensure that neither of these things happen to you. Just like the diet plan, what I'm not going to do is give you a regime to follow – it wouldn't work for everyone and therefore it wouldn't work at all. Instead, I'm going to give you a list of "steps" to follow and some advice that will give you the best possible results for each of these steps. I'm then leaving it up to you to plan the details and carry this out. Why? Because people who set their own exercise schedules are more effective than those who rely on other people to motivate them. This doesn't mean you should cease to work out with other people, go to classes or even get a personal trainer if you can afford it. All of these are great motivators, but if you use them you must ensure that you keep control over why and when you work out. Then, if your friend drops out, the class ends, or your personal trainer moves gyms, your good intentions and everything you've gained so far won't disappear with them.

So What Makes You Stick to a Regime?

STEP ONE: KNOWING WHY YOU ARE DOING IT

Exercise can improve everything from your weight to your sex life, and knowing exactly which benefit you want to tap into with your workout is one of the most important steps in helping you stick to a regime. Below is a list of benefits that exercise can give you. Tick those you think are most important to you, then put them into order of importance.

- Increased energy (1,2,4)
- Decreased stress (1,3,4)
- Improved fitness (1)
- Better body shape (1,2,3)
- Weight gain (2)
- Weight loss (1)
- Decreased body fat (1,2)
- Protection against heart disease/cancer and other major illnesses (1,3,4)
- General improvement of health (1,2,3,4)
- Better sleep patterns (1,3,4)
- Improved relationships (1,3,4)
- Better skin (1,4)
- Higher self-esteem (1,2,3,4)
- Improved longevity (1,4)
- Clearer thinking and better focus (1 ,3 ,4)

STEP TWO: CHOOSING A PLAN THAT REFLECTS YOUR NEEDS

If you don't get the results you want, you'll quit your regime within a few weeks. However, many people don't choose plans that will actually give them the results they want. Different needs obviously respond best to different types of exercise. For example, if you want to increase the health of your heart and lungs there is no point choosing a strength-based regime. Exercise comes in four types, but which regimes work best for what? You'll notice that each of the above benefits is marked with a number. This corresponds to one of the groups below. To devise the dejunked exercise plan, your workout should contain a mixture of all the relevant areas. Obviously, the more a number appears in your list, the more you should work on that area.

TYPE 1: CARDIOVASCULAR: This works your heart and lungs, and includes exercises such as running, walking, swimming, cycling, rowing, skating, dancing and classes like step aerobics. As you'll see, it's probably the most universally beneficial of the four types, affecting everything from clumsiness to longevity (some research has even estimated that every mile someone runs adds four minutes to their life).

TYPE 2: STRENGTH/TONING WORK: This improves muscle definition and tone. It can also be used to increase muscle size. Good methods for this are weight training and toning classes, and weight-based workouts like bodypump.

TYPE 3: STRETCHING: This improves flexibility and decreases tension in the body. Methods like yoga and Pilates emphasize the importance of stretching but it should also be incorporated into the other regimes to decrease risk of injury.

TYPE 4: MENTAL EXERCISES: These use the body to help still and focus the mind. They are often of Eastern origin and include disciplines like tai chi or chi gung. Yoga also falls into this category.

STEP THREE: ... AND FITS YOUR PERSONALITY

If you hate being on your own, it's probably best not to become a long-distance runner. "If an exercise goes against your personality, you are far less likely to stick to it," says Luke Wilkins. "Before you start any exercise programme you should ask yourself a few questions."

HOW IS YOUR SELF-ESTEEM? "One of my clients won't ever do classes because she's too embarrassed by her lack of co-ordination," says Luke. "Despite the fact that I think she'd actually work out more if she did two classes a week, I won't prescribe them to her because I know she won't go for fear of going left when the instructor says go right."

HOW IS YOUR WILL POWER? Do you need a workout buddy, the structure of a class, or the guidance of a trainer to motivate you, or are you motivated enough to work out alone? This one's pretty self-explanatory. If you have no willpower, believing that you're going to let someone down if you don't turn up can be enough to motivate you to work out.

ARE YOU COMPETITIVE? Could you benefit from some of your workout taking place in a sport-orientated environment. If team activities leave you cold, how about entering some of the fun runs that take place round the country?

WHEN DO YOU PREFER TO WORK OUT? Some activities are better suited to mornings or evenings. If you're into really intensive aerobic or strength workouts, it's probably best to be a morning, day or at least very early evening exerciser because these can interfere with sleep.

NOW SET YOURSELF A GOAL
Having a goal is one of the most empowering ways to stick to a regime. Those who have a realistic goal are more likely to stick to an exercise plan than those who have nothing to aim for. It's also really important to write that aim down. Goals that you put on paper are far more likely to be realized than those that exist only in your mind. Just ensure that anything you put down is realistic in terms of the time you have and your level of fitness. "The second reason most people drop out of exercise is that they try and do too much too soon and find things hard to stick to," says Luke Wilkins. "Whatever your goal is, make it realistic and attainable in the time you've set yourself. You should be pushing yourself but not exhausting yourself. Generally trying to raise your speed, your distance or your intensity by about 10 per cent every week or so is a good goal. If you're training for something big like a marathon, aim for little steps – two miles, three miles and so on." One word of warning. While weight loss is often a great motivator for people to start exercising, it's not the best reason to have in your head. "To lose weight by exercise alone takes about six hours of moderately fast running a week," says Luke Wilkins. "That's extremely hard for people to stick to. The ideal balance for weight loss is that 80 per cent of the effort should come from changing your diet and the final 20 should be achieved by exercise. Also, while you're doing this exercise, forget about the weight-loss goal and concentrate on something like being able to run a mile faster – or being able to run two miles instead of one. The more you aim towards that, the more energy you'll burn and weight loss will come."

STEP FOUR: GETTING STARTED
If you've never exercised before, this is the hardest step. "The first time I exercised, I went puce," says 34-year-old website designer Rhian. "I went running with two colleagues who had done the marathon and I nearly died when they had to stop and wait for me, but every run after that got easier and now I run about 25 miles a week." Remember that everyone has to start somewhere: five minutes is better than nothing.

HOW DO YOU MOTIVATE YOURSELF TO WORK OUT?

- "I just tell myself that I've done it before and so I'll do it again. If I don't do at least what I did last week, I feel as if I've been beaten." Andrew, 39, composer

- "I have a written-down training programme which I stick to religiously – it helps that I'm running a marathon and if I don't do it this way I'll never get to the end, which will just be extremely embarrassing." Jane, 30, sub-editor

- "I tell myself I only have to do ten minutes – however, at about nine minutes the feel-good factor starts to kick in and so I always carry on. If I get to ten minutes and I still hate it I know that's a day when I really do need a rest." Thomas, 42, managing director

- "I don't mind the exercising, it's all the getting changed, etc. afterwards that I hate – so on days when I don't want to go I put my gym stuff on under my clothes before I leave. I then tell myself that I don't have to have a shower afterwards and I just chuck my coat over my kit – it's disgusting but for some reason it works." Kelly, 27, adminstration executive.

Seven Other Ways to Maximize Your Health

1 TAKE A DAILY MULTIVITAMIN

The argument rages on about the levels of nutrients we need in a day – and whether we can get them all from food. In reality, few of us eat enough different sorts of food to achieve maximum health – and those we do eat are, by virtue of chemical processing, intensive farming or extended transportation times, less nutritious than we think. Taking a multivitamin is like a security net. Beware, though, many of the tablets on the market use substandard ingredients or skimp on quantities. To find a good-quality pill takes two tests. Read the label and check the quantities – a good-quality, high potency vitamin will contain at least 50 mg of each B vitamin, 200 mg of vitamin C and 15 mg of zinc. These are the most expensive to process and hence the first to be reduced in quality or quantity. The second test checks how well your vitamin will absorb in your body. Drop a pill into a small quantity of vinegar. If it dissolves within 20 minutes, it'll do the same in your body.

2 CHEW YOUR FOOD PROPERLY

If you don't help your body break down a food, not only will the nutrients you absorb be fewer (possibly by as much as half) but you'll also use up more energy which will leave you fatigued – not the point of eating your healthy dejunked diet at all.

3 DETOX YOUR HOME

The average home contains a cocktail of over 150 chemicals. These may originate from cleaning fluids or even MDF, a fibre used in the production of many kitchen cupboards. The possible effects of this chemical cocktail include respiratory disorders, skin problems and fatigue. To minimize exposure, reduce the use of chemical-based cleaning products and electrical appliances which emit radiation. Leaving your windows open for an hour a day will help disperse build-up – if you live in a polluted area, don't panic: experts believe constant exposure to the chemicals in our homes is actually more harmful than any exposure caused by opening windows. You should also fill your home with plants such as spider plants and Chinese evergreens, which have been proven to absorb chemicals from the air.

4 GET THE RIGHT AMOUNT OF SLEEP FOR YOUR BODY

Both sleeping too much and sleeping too little have detrimental effects on your health. To determine your own personal sleep prescription you should spend two weeks listening to your body. Sleep when you're tired, get up when you wake. Make a note of how much you have slept and add up the total for the fortnight. Divide this by 14 and you'll discover the amount you need to sleep each night. But what if you can't sleep? Insomnia affects millions of people across the world every night. The most common causes are stress (which we tackle throughout the book) and environmental factors. "An uncomfortable bed can dramatically decrease the amount of hours you sleep in a night," says the National Bed Federation. Other factors that can affect your sleep include temperature (the ideal bedroom temperature should be about 65 degrees) and noise. Constant background noise disturbs sleep quality, intermittent noise leads to disrupted sleep. Both add up to one grumpy person the morning after. Rooms should be kept as quiet as possible – and if noise is a constant problem try a white-noise machine. Finally, watch out for light. Blinds should be as dark as possible.

5 KEEP THE NOISE DOWN

We mentioned it in the sleep section, but noise while you're awake is also bad for your health. Too much noise leads to increased heart rate, raised blood pressure and irritability. People exposed to constant noise are more prone to bad tempers and stress reactions such as ulcers. To reduce damage, you need half an hour's silence every day.

6 BREATHE CORRECTLY

Our lungs can take in the equivalent of a litre bottle's worth of air every breath – most of us treat them to about a glassful. Not breathing correctly leads to fatigue, increases stress and messes with your skin. The best way to breathe is through your mouth and from your diaphragm. How do you tell if you're doing things correctly? Place one hand on your stomach and one on your chest and breathe in. If the hand on your stomach rises, all is good; if it's the one on your chest, you're unlikely to be taking in everything you need. One good way to learn to breathe correctly – and reduce stress – is to learn to blow bubbles with soapy water (remember how you used to do that as a kid?). To blow the perfect bubble, you have to breathe out more slowly than you breathed in. This is the key to perfect breath control.

7 DRINK WATER

When we're dehydrated, our body functions at half-power. We can't move as fast as normal, either mentally or physically, and our looks suffer. We get tired and irritable. The average person needs at least two litres of water a day to detox their system. If you choose to take in yours through bottled water you'll also increase your vitamin levels. One litre of a calcium-rich water can provide up to a sixth of the recommended daily amount of this vital nutrient for women. If bottled water busts your budget, filtered tap water is okay, but from the cold tap.

Timesaver tip: The thirty-minute gym workout

While studies have shown that ten-minute bursts of running and walking help you lose weight, some of us prefer to exercise in one long burst – but how can you maximize effects and minimize time?

THE EXERCISES

"While you shouldn't use this plan every workout (your body quickly adapts to exercise and you should vary workouts all the time), if you're time-pushed, this workout is better than no workout at all," says Luke Wilkins. "If you're doing a short workout, it can be tempting to concentrate just on cardiovascular (CV) work or toning, but for a completely rounded workout you should do both. Circuit training is the best way to fit a great workout in a short time. Do five minutes warm-up cycling. From then on, alternate five minutes' hard CV work on any machine with two strength/toning exercises. You are aiming to do twenty to thirty reps of each, working at a weight that feels too hard at about 28 reps. Work quite fast but watch your technique to ensure you're using the right muscles, not just aimlessly pushing the weight. Don't leave a gap between machines, keep your heart rate up. In total, you're aiming for fifteen minutes' fast aerobic work, seven minutes' strength work, five minutes' warm-up, three minutes' cool-down stretching."

Summary

Your body is made up of everything you've put into it in the last twelve months

The number of toxins that enter our bodies mean that most of us don't function effectively

The side-effects of this include fatigue, decreased immunity, allergies, digestive disorders, stress problems

Most of us need to dejunk and doing so can help the physical, mental and emotional areas of our lives

Exercise is vital for a healthy, dejunked life

No one exercise plan fits all – no one diet fits all. We do not all need eight hours of sleep. For optimum health you need to work out your personal requirements for everything that benefits you

Action Plan

Find out how much you need to dejunk and which areas of your life are creating the most toxicity

Try the detox plan that's best for you

Work out your ideal diet and start to integrate it into your life. If you find it hard to change everything at once, start by getting refined carbohydrate and fat levels under control. The rest will then become much easier to implement

Work out your personal exercise prescription

Take the first exercise step and then form an exercise pattern for each day/week. Use the motivational tools to keep you going for six weeks. Most experts say that once you incorporate something regularly into your life for six weeks, it becomes a habit – and habits are hard to break

Check out the other health-sappers in your life. Look at your vitamin intake, your sleep patterns, your breathing, etc. Make maximizing your health a priority for at least one month (the shortest amount of time it takes to start seeing and feeling results), then assess how things have changed. Look at things like energy levels, your outward appearance, your mood and reactions to stress and other outside stimuli. Do you now feel okay – or do you feel good? At the very least, you should feel better

Chapter 4
Dejunk Your Time

TIME, MONEY AND WORK lead to dissatisfaction for billions of people in the modern world. We want more time, less work and more money, yet society demands exactly the opposite, filling our lives with conflict. These three practical areas of our existence determine how we feel about the rest of our lives, and time and time again studies have revealed negative links.

The time-overload to which we subject ourselves is now immense. According to the Henley Centre for Forecasting, the amount of free time we have decreased by 10 per cent between 1985 and 1995 – and that decline is expected to continue. Part of the decline is due to the heavily work-orientated society that we live in. According to the Institute of Management, average middle managers are now working ten hours more a week than they did in 1985 just to keep their heads above water. But another huge part is due to the fact that, just as we judge ourselves by what we have, we judge ourselves by what we do. How many times is this the first question you ask when you meet someone at a party? We have developed into a race of people who believe that if we immerse ourselves in a world of frenetic busyness we are actually worth more.

Time surveys have revealed that while the average man has five hours a day when he could do something completely for himself, women have three hours. Yet few of us actually use the time in this way. It's been quoted that 65 per cent of our leisure time is spent doing things that we do not want to do, and a recent study by the British Heart Foundation revealed that over 50 per cent of 25–30-year-old workers are taking just half an hour for lunch in a working day – just long enough to cram down a sandwich at their desks. Instead of taking time out to refresh our bodies and minds, the average evening is spent cleaning, cooking, catching up on the bills and then vegging out in front of the TV – none of which actually allows us to recharge effectively. To benefit our minds and therefore our bodies, we need to create at least thirty minutes of "me-time" every day. Me-time is anything you do purely for your pleasure. It's not bathing because you're trying to get clean, or snatching five minutes with kids because otherwise they'll forget who you are, or eating out with friends you don't really like because you haven't seen them for a while. It's taking a totally self-indulgent aromatherapy bath until the water goes cold; it's spending a night sleeping in a tent in the garden with the children, just because it's fun. It's eating out with people you love in a restaurant you really want to visit. And at least once a week, it's half an hour sitting in a quiet, relaxing place and just thinking about nothing.

But That's Impossible to Fit into My Life . . .

No, it's not. It's just not something we're used to thinking about – and it's certainly not something we think of prioritizing. There are two simple ways to create more time –

we can physically make more time and we can mentally find more time – and the next few pages are going to teach you how to do both.

How to Make More Time

Most of our time overload is caused by tasks – be it our job, our personal paperwork and household chores, or physical necessities like cooking and shopping for food. But in fact much of the time we spend on these areas of our lives is actually grossly unnecessary. Almost anyone who's ever uttered the phrase "I haven't got enough time" could make more time if they reorganized the practical stuff they do in their day-to-day lives. "Many people spend their days in a frenzy of activity but achieve very little because they are not concentrating on the right things," says James Manktelow from Mind Tools (an internet advice service). "To successfully overcome the time overload in which we now live, we should concentrate on getting results rather than just being busy."

STEP ONE: DETERMINE YOUR TIME PERSONALITY

Most of us have an established way of dealing with things that ensures we do – or more often don't – get things done. Experts call this your time personality. "And knowing which time personality category you fall into and understanding the strengths and weaknesses of that personality can make you more efficient," says Stephanie Denton, president of Ohio-based organizing company Denton and Co. "By identifying your time personality you could save 15–20 per cent of your daily working time."

Take a look at the following groups of statements and pinpoint the group that reflects your attitude to tasks best. When you've determined which, read on to identify your personality and how you should tackle it.

TYPE 1: I find it hard to start certain tasks and often leave things until I absolutely have to do them

There is always one day a week when I end up doing a whole day of tasks I hate

I can be easily distracted from a task I don't want to do

I tidy my workspace at least three times a day

TYPE 2: I spend a lot of time trying to find the tools I need to complete a task

I find it hard to determine priorities and often have to switch tasks halfway through

I find it easy to work in a messy environment

I like people to know if I'm busy

TYPE 3: I often spend time doing things I don't want to do or that my partner or workmates should be doing

Whenever I get control of my time, someone gives me something else to do

I spend more time helping others than I do doing what I need to get done

I worry what others will think of me and need to be liked

TYPE 4: I hate giving things to other people to do – they never do it properly

I spend a lot of time on details

I rarely feel proud of things that I have done

Everything in my life has a place and everything is in its place

TYPE 5: I always start the day organized but never seem to get everything done

Other people never seem to understand how important things are – or how quickly I need them

Simple jobs always seem to take longer than they should

I'm always apologizing to my friends for being late

Once you have decided which type you are ... read on.

TYPE 1

You're a procrastinator. Your time overload is not caused by the amount of work you have to do but by the fact that you can't get started fast enough. This saps time in two ways. Things build up and jobs that should have taken five minutes take an hour; also, you end up starting tasks later than you should so that time that should have been part of the working day eats into your private time.

THE FOUR RULES FOR PROCRASTINATORS

LOOK AT WHY YOU PROCRASTINATE. "This is often caused by lack of confidence in your abilities, boredom/dislike of what you have to do or a task that's just too big," says Stephanie Denton. "The absolute first way of dealing with procrastination is to determine why you are doing it – and then try to solve the problems at the source." Things to ask yourself are, would someone else enjoy the tasks you find mundane – and are you able to delegate to them? If you're procrastinating on big tasks, low self-confidence is often the cause. Ask yourself what you're afraid of and tackle it.

DO THINGS YOU DON'T WANT TO DO FIRST EVERY DAY. Once they're out of the way, the rest of your day will be more productive.

IF YOU FIND IT HARD TO DEAL WITH BIG TASKS, BREAK THEM INTO PIECES. Then set a deadline for each – and stick to it. "Sometimes it can help to get someone else to start a task," says Stephanie Denton. "It just gets you started."

USE A REWARD SYSTEM. Treat yourself once you've completed something you really didn't want to do. "It sounds simple but it really does motivate you to do things," says Stephanie.

TYPE 2

You're a disorganizer and your time overload is caused by spending most of your day trying to find the tools you need or hopping between jobs because you didn't realize things were so urgent. "Many disorganizers work this way because they subconsciously believe that a messy desk or other work area and harassed air signifies to people that they are busy and therefore indispensable," says Allison Van Norman. "Sadly, the opposite is usually the case."

The Ideal Time Chart

Once you've created all these new hours in your day, you need to ensure you're not filling them with more stuff you don't want to do. To keep you on track, make some time circles. Get yourself a pen and paper. On the paper draw two circles. In circle one draw a pie chart estimating what percentage of your time is spent

• working

• with family/friends

• actively relaxing

• doing things you enjoy

• sleeping

• on general household and other mundane/obligatory tasks

In the next circle draw a chart to represent how much time you would like to spend on those areas of your life – compare the two and work on making that ideal reality.

THE FOUR RULES FOR DISORGANIZERS

KNOW YOUR FAULTS AND GET A SYSTEM THAT DEALS WITH THEM. When you've finished using something, put it back where it should go. If you lose telephone numbers, get a huge address book and write down every number you think you might ever need again (work contacts, plumbers, whatever). If you're writing an appointment in your diary, write contact numbers and addresses on the page. If everything is in one place you can't lose it.

DEJUNK YOUR WORKSPACE. The professional desk contains those items only immediately applicable to the task at hand – everything else should be filed or in the bin. This should apply to every task you do – if you're doing the ironing you don't need to fight through piles of dirty clothes to get to the clean ones.

SPEND THE LAST TEN MINUTES OF YOUR DAY ORGANIZING YOURSELF FOR THE NEXT. Write a "to do" list and a plan. Time-planning company Walpole believe that disorganizers can complete things at least a fifth faster if they have a day plan. Planning may also help you achieve better results. A study at Seneca College found that students who planned their work were much more likely to have A and B grades than those who didn't plan things.

TOUCH EVERYTHING ONLY ONCE. The average person handles 300 pieces of paper a day and each of them will pass through their hands five times before they tackle it – and you wonder why you don't get to sit down to dinner till 8 p.m. Whenever a piece of paper arrives on your desk or in your home, you should use one of the three D's. Either deal with it, dump it or delegate it. (This is explained in more detail in chapter 1. If you've skipped straight here, head back there for more ideas.)

TYPE 3

You're an overloader. Chances are you're the most popular person you know. Why? Because you just can't say no. As well as your own tasks you're taking on those of your boss and your partner or friends. "The first problem here is you don't want people to dislike you and often it's easier to say yes than offend," says Stephanie Denton. "But also, people often take on too much because they haven't identified their goals and priorities. How can you determine what you should be doing if you don't know where it's taking you?"

THE FOUR RULES FOR OVERLOADERS

LEARN TO SAY NO. It's the most fundamental rule but it can often be the hardest. "Saying no is not always bad," says Stephanie Denton. "There are ways of turning people down that can be positive. Suggest alternative ways of dealing with a situation – someone else who may be able to help, for example. If this is someone you really don't want to offend, say you can't work on it immediately but say you'll do it when you're less busy. 'Which will be . . .' That leaves it up to them to determine if that's soon enough."

GET RID OF SOME OF YOUR OWN TASKS. Sometimes, what you're being asked to do is more interesting than your own work. If this is the case, decide if everything you're doing currently is necessary and if you should be the one doing it.

ASK WHAT EACH TASK YOU TAKE ON IS DOING FOR YOU. Next time you're asked to add to your workload, think what you'll get out of it. Will it fulfil you, teach you something new, or help you in some way? If the answer is "no", don't do it.

WORK ON YOUR FEELINGS OF CONFIDENCE AND GUILT. "Poor time-planning is not the problem with overloaders, poor self-image is," says Stephanie Denton.

TYPE 4
You're a perfectionist and the reason you're overloaded is that you can't let responsibilities, standards or tasks you're working on, go. Most of your fine-tuning is unnecessary.

THE THREE RULES FOR PERFECTIONISTS

SHARE TASKS OUT TO OTHERS. If it makes you feel better, make it easy tasks, while you concentrate on the tough stuff, but if you really want to overcome this pressure you'll have to give tasks to everyone. Delegate, but set an early deadline so you have time to fine-tune; just remember that this is all you are doing – you're not starting again from scratch.

KNOW WHEN TO LET GO. As soon as you finish a job and have checked it once, put your tools away. If it needs to go to someone else, send it there immediately.

How We Spend Our Time at Home Each Day

66 minutes cleaning

49 minutes personal grooming

34 minutes cooking meals

25 minutes playing with children

25 minutes playing with pets

15 minutes exercising

How We Spend Our Working Lives

Five years reading and writing letters

Four years commuting

Three years on the telephone

Two years in meetings

One year in the lavatory

Eleven months looking for things we've lost

Six months reading junk mail

Ten months personal phonecalls

LOOK AT THE WORKING METHODS OF THOSE YOU RESPECT. How do yours compare? If you are overworking, you'll see.

TYPE 5

You're an underestimator and the reason you're working late is that you try and do too much in too little time. "Most jobs take at least twice as long as we think they're going to," says Stephanie Denton. "I'd say 99 per cent of people fall into this group in some way. If you get to the end of your day and you have only done two things on your day list, yet you've been working really hard, it should tell you something."

THE THREE RULES FOR UNDERESTIMATORS

HAVE THREE THINGS ON YOUR "TO DO" LIST. Ensure your list is realistic. You can always do more than is on the list – but you won't feel bad about doing less.

ACTUALLY MEASURE HOW LONG IT TAKES YOU TO DO COMMON TASKS. Then compare this with how long you thought they would take.

SET EARLY DEADLINES. You won't end up stressed out if you do overrun.

STEP TWO: SPOT YOUR PERSONAL TIME-SAPPERS

Now you know how to deal with personality-induced time overload, you'll have the background to deal with the other nightmares that turn an eight-hour day into an eighty-hour week. Time managers believe up to a fifth of our task time is wasted time – but the time-sappers can be easy to spot.

Take 26-year-old Anna, for example. She's a trainee actuary. She's smart, she's successful and she's seriously pressed for time and doesn't know why. Generally, she gets into her office at 7.30 a.m. and gets home at 8 p.m. laden with work. "I don't think I waste much time in my day but no matter what I do I still end up putting in a twelve-hour day." In a case like this, chances are it's little things that are attacking Anna's timings. Little things like how many interruptions she gets from colleagues, how long she spends on the phone and how long she spends reading e-mails. We asked Anna to keep a diary for three days. This revealed a lot – she scored points for her use of delegation, for taking a half-hour lunch break out of the building every day and her distinct lack of personal calls. But we did work out that she was wasting about twenty hours a week on common time-sappers. By correcting these, she managed to leave work on time three days a week and get all her studying done.

ANNA'S MAIN TIME-SAPPERS

PERSONAL CHAT: 10 hours wasted a week

While talking to colleagues is one of the things that makes the day pleasant, Anna loses a lot of time through being sociable. However, it's not so much during working hours that she suffers but when she works late to study. One evening, Anna stayed at work till 8.15 – two and a quarter hours after her allotted home time. During this time she spent half an hour studying, half an hour drafting a letter that needed to be sent and one and half hours chatting over personal things or work that needed to be actioned the following day.

When the work day finishes, it can be easy for everyone to slacken off and the amount of time devoted to chat can easily surpass your good intentions. Anna finds it easier to study away from home as she has a little girl who demands her attention at home – but perhaps her colleagues are also demanding too much attention at work. Management consultant Mary Horsnell suggested Anna take her work to the local library two evenings a week. "It means you can't be distracted. What's more, our mind associates different environments with different activities – the reason you find it so hard to study in a bedroom, for example. By going to the library, an environment Anna also associates with study, her mind will switch into retain mode and take more in." Anna took Mary's advice and got four times as much work done.

E-MAIL AND VOICEMAIL: 3 hours wasted a week

While Anna scores serious time-saver points by switching her phone to voicemail while she works, she checks either her voicemail or her e-mail an average of every half an hour – and responds immediately to all requests. Not only does this waste time, it also interrupts her train of thought, which slows things down. She's not alone; in a recent survey of managers it was estimated that e-mail is actually turning into one of the biggest time-sappers in the modern office environment.

Timesaver Tip: E-mail

Only check e-mail and voicemail three times a day. The best times are first thing, after lunch and an hour before home. These are usually natural breaks in the day and allow you to respond to those requests that are urgent before you leave for home – and schedule the other responses for first thing the next day. "If you develop a system and pattern for responding to calls, people will understand this and work around it," says Stephanie Denton

POOR PHONE TECHNIQUE: estimated 2 hours wasted a week

Experts believe it takes five minutes of goodwill chat to pass on a piece of information – and Anna is definitely falling prey to this. "Most of my calls are reacting to my voicemail and are generally to provide a figure for a client or a fact that they need. However, invariably I end up chatting about other areas of their account which just ends up with my needing to find out more information."

Timesaver Tip: Fax

The fax! If your client isn't on e-mail and you don't want to risk not catching their voicemail, the fax can be a godsend. Dropping a note containing the relevant information ensures you've provided what's needed but prevents you getting caught in a chat zone. You can always lie and say the phone was engaged. You shouldn't use this all the time, but in time-crunched days it really helps. One leading businesswoman also only returns fact-based calls from her home phone after hours. "Their voicemail is on and I save hours of time," she reveals.

WORKING ON TOO MUCH AT ONCE: 4 hours wasted a week

At any one time, Anna is working with five or six clients at once. However, she has a tendency to skip from account to account. The problem with this is that when your mind switches from one thing to another there's a time lag while you stop thinking about one thing and start concentrating effectively on the next. "I do think it takes me three or four minutes to remember where I am on something and find everything I need, which is annoying if I'm then only working on something for twenty or thirty minutes."

Timesaver Tip: Time plan

Anna is lucky because she has a polychronic personality, which means she can handle more than one thing at once. Without this, the transference time between tasks would dramatically slow her down. However, she does suffer a little from disorganization and as such she would be better off consolidating her work at the beginning and end of every day so that she completes all her work for one client in one go. A time plan would help here. "She should also have a checklist attached to each file," says Mary Horsnell. "This would allow her to put things into context more easily – and pick up immediately where she left off."

PANIC MOMENTS: 1 hour wasted a week

At least three times a week Anna has what she calls a "faffing moment". "It's one of those times when I walk aimlessly round the office trying to work out what to do next – I don't know how to deal with this as I don't think I'm naturally disorganized."

> ## Timesaver Tip: Tension release
>
> *"I don't actually think Anna needs to do too much about these. Taking a few moments to regroup our thoughts can be extremely beneficial," says osteopath Mike Evans. "But maybe she should use the time more therapeutically. Shrugging the tension from her shoulders, taking a five-minute break outside, or even just doodling for two or three minutes between jobs can help clear and refresh your mind and would help Anna refocus instead of panic."*

How to Make Your Own Activity Log

We chose Anna's workday because most people will find it's worktime that contains time-sappers – but most of the principles can be applied to your home life. When 37-year-old marketing manager Sean carried it out in the evening, for example, he found that he spent half an hour each evening clearing up stuff he'd not put away that morning. By not shopping effectively he spent three nights a week queuing in the supermarket and at least an hour a week talking to people he didn't want to on the phone. "By switching on my answerphone so my boss couldn't find me, by writing a shopping list every week, and by tidying up as I went along every morning, I managed to save at least an hour every night," he explains. To make your own activity log, note down the things you do every day for three days without changing your behaviour at all. Every time you change activities, whether opening mail, reading e-mails, making coffee or gossiping, note down the time of the change (to the second). Once you've got the results, you should look at things like:

• **How long you are spending on things compared with how long you** *think* **you are spending**

• **The amount of time you spend relative to the importance of the task; on this basis, you can establish where you should be cutting back on the time you devote to tasks**

Timesaver Tip: The five-minute phone call

Phone calls are one of the biggest office and personal time-sappers. Mindtools pinpoint the following tips to keep calls professional and to the point:

- *Have an aim: know what you want to discuss and have everything to hand*

- *Limit social conversation: don't be unfriendly, but don't linger on chat*

- *Give concise answers to questions you are asked: it's a natural human response to echo the style of the person you are talking to. If you're concise, the person you are calling should be too*

- *Don't be afraid to say you'll call someone back. If you don't know the answer to a question or if you really can't talk, say so, but always return the call*

How to Find Time in Your Day

By following all the steps above, you could save many hours a week to spend on whatever you want. Whether it's more time with your family, time to start exercising or time just to sit and do nothing (which is time we should all get far more used to spending). However, making time isn't the only way you can grab time to do things or relax. Everybody's day has at least half an hour of what we'll call "deadtime", scrap seconds that you can use to chill out or do something simple like paying a bill or cleaning out a drawer.

Deadtime is time that you probably refer to at the moment as wasted time – you'll generally recognize it by its ability to make you sigh, tut, look at your watch or mutter "come on", under your breath. However, from now on you'll refer to this time as "found time". It's like finding a five-pound note in your pocket. You wouldn't look at that and think, "I wasted that when I put it in my pocket and forgot all about it." You'd think, "Oh, look, extra cash," and that's how you should react to found time.

So where are these mythical minutes in our lives?

TRAVEL TIME

Experts say that half an hour of uninterrrupted worktime is the equivalent of one hour in the office. Use travel time to dictate letters or write notes; or use it to relax totally; the motion of a moving train can be very relaxing. I use travel time to return phone calls. At the end of my daily journey to work, I have a ten-minute walk and so I call people.

How to Have a More Productive Day, Whatever You Do

MAKE A "TO DO" LIST. People who do this get much more work done than less organized workers. Just one thing – would a daily list be good for you, or a weekly one? If you're working on a lot of big projects, a weekly list might be better

ONLY EVER PUT THREE THINGS ON YOUR "TO DO" LIST. You'll always get everything done and you could end up doing more

DON'T DO THE EASY STUFF FIRST. Yes, it makes for a neatly crossed-off list, but normally by the time you get to the end of the simple stuff you haven't got time to deal with the tough stuff. Instead, you should mark the list in order of priority and work through it that way

MAKE THE ONE CALL THAT'S BUGGING YOU. If one task keeps popping into your mind, do it – urgent or not. You won't feel as if you've done anything until you've dealt with that one

KNOW YOUR ENERGY CYCLES (and how to adapt them). We all function on different biological clocks – some of us are morning people, some evening. Identify your prime time and plan to spend it on your most creative thinking and most demanding jobs whenever possible

HAVE MEETINGS IN THE MORNING. Morning meetings are always shorter. People are more creative and also want to get on with their own work. If you schedule a meeting at the end of the day, people often see it as the last thing they do and will drag it out until home time

AND THEN MAKE YOUR PHONE CALLS. According to British Telecom, peak phone load periods are 10 a.m., 1–2 p.m. and 4 p.m.

APPOINTMENT TIME

Waiting for someone to see you is perfect me-time. You probably don't want to be seen doing anything else in case they think you're unprepared, so it's time to relax. You can make some significant mental gains in just two minutes. One excellent exercise here is palming – place your hands over your eyes, blocking out all the light for a few minutes. Don't push on your eyes: just rest your palms over them. This reduces stimuli to the brain and calms your nerves.

TECHNO TIME

The few minutes it takes for your computer to turn on in the morning or the seconds while you wait for something to print are peppered with de-stress time. Some experts say for every twenty minutes you work, you should stretch for twenty seconds, which fits perfectly into techno time. You can also fill this time with mini tasks. "I've put my in-tray, chequebook, envelopes and stamps next to the kettle," says 49-year-old personal assistant Raksha. "While I'm waiting for it to boil, I pay a bill or send off a form. Small tasks never really get a chance to build up that way."

DOZING TIME

The half-hour lie-in may be pleasant, but it doesn't do anything to decrease your sleep debt or your stress levels. Getting up when you wake up can add thirty minutes to your day – that's an extra week of "me-time" a year.

QUEUING TIME

You really shouldn't stress out about waiting in line – researchers at Duke University in North Carolina discovered that people who stress about simple, easy things like the fact that the queue next door is moving faster are between four and seven times more likely to die early. Instead, you should use queuing time as scrap second time. Make personal calls, try palming, or even use that time to read articles you've torn out of magazines and newspapers and kept in your wallet or purse. However you use the scrap seconds, don't stress it: you'll never die in the queue, but you might die because of it!

Summary

The amount of free time we have in our lives is decreasing at a rate of around 10 per cent a year

This leads to a myriad of health and emotional problems

Spending just thirty minutes a day solely on yourself is all it takes to prevent this damage

We do have time for this in our lives; we just aren't used to prioritizing it

Knowing your time personality can save a fifth of your working day

Knowing our time-sappers can save another fifth

Everybody has at least thirty minutes of deadtime in their day. Learning how to focus on this time and use it productively can help us make time elsewhere in our lives

Action Plan

Do the ideal time chart so you know how different your time ideal is from the reality and just how much time you need to free up in your day

Look at your time personality and implement the tips

Fill in your activity log. Analyse what your most common time-sappers are and how you can deal with them

Carry out a scrap-seconds audit. Ask yourself if you would find it more beneficial to relax during these mini-breaks or whether you should use them for small tasks, freeing up time later in the day

Use your free time well. Take another look at your ideal time chart or cross off some of the things from the list you made in Chapter 1. Only once you start enjoying your free time will you realize how much benefit it can give. What's more, once your health and mental processes have benefited from a release of pressure, you could find you manage to make even more time for yourself

Chapter 5
Dejunk Your Finances

IT'S ESTIMATED THAT *within the next fifteen years most people will be living a simpler life. We won't want so many possessions, we won't get so excited when our promotion brings with it a bigger car and we won't care how much we earn. We'll finally realize that money really doesn't buy happiness. We earn more now than ever before but lifestyle studies show our happiness levels peaked in 1957! However, until all around us develop this higher state of consciousness, most of us will continue to shop till we drop in an attempt to buy ourselves a better life. The trouble is that none of us has really got the balance right. Between 1995 and 1996 the number of Americans who worried about money increased by 12 per cent, yet earnings didn't decrease during this time. The British are equally as cash concerned. The more we earn, the more we spend; the more we get used to spending, the more we feel we can't ever live with less money – and the less satisfied with our lives we become.*

Whitney had fallen into this trap completely. She was vice-president of a small mortgage company and was clearing about $8,000 (£5,000) a month. Rapid expansion of the company had left her seriously overworked and unhappy. "I dreaded going to work each day. Once I was there I would either get angry or cry – or both. I used to wish that I could get really, really sick or hit by a truck or something equally as disastrous so I would be forced into hospital for time off. I was not a pleasant person. I ate, breathed and slept that job, and my only topic of conversation was the problems I was having at work, but no other job would pay me that much money and I was stuck."

The truth is, financial freedom was within Whitney's grasp and it is within yours. It is possible to cut your wages without dramatically interfering with your standard of living. It is possible to get out of debt. It is possible to make more money without working every single hour of every single day and, if you really want to, it is possible to give it all up and move to the country (or another country). And this is what dejunking teaches you. Whitney finally managed it. "A couple of other guys were also miserable and we'd talked about setting up on our own – then the crunch came. It was my daughter's birthday and I'd told my boss that I couldn't work late – but five minutes before quitting time a new loan came in and I was told I would have to stay until it was complete and he didn't care whose birthday it was.

"Two months later my partners and I had sorted out everything and we resigned. We started May 1998 and by early 1999 we were starting to show a little profit. I'd effectively cut my income in half but I still met my bills and my mortgage. It is hard because I'm a single mother and telling my girls they couldn't have something because money was tight that month was tough, but I knew it wasn't for ever. I felt the money I was earning before was blood money, but now I no longer feel as if I'm going to explode and I'm in control of my stressors. I actually have fun at work. I've learned that making less money at a job you love is more important than making a lot of money at a job you hate – life is too short to be miserable for a third of each day."

Whitney is unusual in that she managed to live her dream. Time and time again, studies reveal that most workers would take a pay cut for more flexible hours, or that they would trade a day's pay for a day off. The more people earn, the more likely it is that they want to do this. Yet only one-third of American workers and one-sixth of British workers have actually made any move towards redressing the stress/cash balance. Dejunking your money is not so much about changing how much money you have but about changing your attitudes to it – which in most cases will actually lead to increased pennies in your pocket. Life management coach Robin Chandler says, "Money isn't a problem, people just have problems with it." Many of us worry incessantly about money when there really is no need. We are not starving, we are not going to lose our home, we just can't have all those things that we want and that's where you start to readjust things.

Dejunking your money can be done in three ways. You can dramatically change your standard of living so that you do not need to earn so much money. You can decrease the amount of money that you expend (notice I didn't say spend here; dejunking your money does not mean you have to go without, it's just a matter of shifting priorities, as I'll explain later). Finally, you can increase the amount of money coming in. So, which of these is the best method for you?

The Change Your Life Plan (or how to earn less and spend less)

Generally, you'll know if you want to use this method. This is not a little change, this is a full-on, downshift your life situation. It's for you if you have a dream to free yourself from financial chains for ever. Perhaps you don't want to work at all any more or you want to downscale your hours dramatically to spend more time at home; you may even want to plough money into some kind of venture of your own. It's the dream of many people, but could you actually do it? The answer is probably yes. Many of us are worth a lot more than we think and when the trappings of daily life are removed, we actually don't need that much to get by. Giving up the nine to nine grind is probably easier than you think – some of you could even do it tomorrow. In fact, the first step to long-term financial freedom is to determine what would happen if you did decide to up sticks tomorrow. Would you sink or swim? The way to do this is by finding out exactly how much you're worth.

STEP ONE: THE NASTY BIT
It's time to work out what you owe. Calculate absolutely everything you owe in life. Include:

- Bank (or other) loans and overdrafts
- Credit card/store card debts
- Anything you owe family and friends
- Unpaid bills
- Balance on your mortgage
- Balance on your car loan
- Anything left to pay on HP agreements

STEP TWO: HOW RICH ARE YOU?

Add up all of your assets. This should include:

- Cash (what's in the bank, your purse and your piggy bank)
- Savings accounts
- The current sale value of your home and your car
- Money owed to you by family, friends or any other debtors
- The current surrender value (i.e. if you cashed them in tomorrow) of any investments, pensions, saving plans, life policies, shares, etc

STEP THREE: WHAT HAVE YOU BOUGHT?

Now go through your home and work out what you'd get if you sold everything you own – fixtures, fittings, gadgets, clothes, jewellery, all of it. Don't think, "But I wouldn't sell it," just value it. Add this to your assets.

STEP FOUR: TAKE WHAT YOU OWE AWAY FROM WHAT YOU OWN

This gives your financial profile. You may find that if you sold all your excess possessions, got rid of the car and cashed in a few of those policies that ensure you'll be all right in ten years' time, you could actually do what you wanted to do with your life right now.

If things don't look so good, you'll need to analyse where to cut back. First, look at what you hope to do with your life. How much is this really going to cost you and can you adapt this in any way to cut those costs? Remember, changing your life will change your needs. If you want to give up work, you won't need so much money for clothing or travel, for example. If you're not travelling day in day out to your place of work, could you move further away? Or go somewhere smaller and cheaper? Will things like the council tax or house insurance decrease if you move? Look at what changes downshifting will bring and what it'll take for you to afford them. If you're still lacking funds, determine what you need to do to redress the balance and take steps towards that. The following Save Plan will probably help.

The Save Plan (or how to get by on less money without living like a pauper)

If you like the idea of getting by on less money but don't like the idea of changing your standard of living too much – this is the method for you. What it aims to do is cut the amount you are spending each month without making a dramatic difference to your lifestyle. The truth is, many of us waste an awful lot of money, most of which we don't even notice. For example, we overheat our houses: lowering the thermostat on your heating by just one degree will save you 5 per cent on your heating bill a year. Most of us use 50 per cent more toothpaste, shampoo, shaving foam, etc. than we really need. Cutting back to the recommended levels of this would save the average shopper about £15 a year. You're probably looking at that and thinking, why bother? Because these are two examples – there are probably 100 others that you could carry out every year of your life, saving you anything from £1 to £100 every time. All these together will soon add up. It's like a dripping tap – one drip makes no difference but by the time the tap has dripped for a day you've wasted a bucket full of water. By plugging the cash drips in your home, you can help reduce your debts, increase your savings or simply change the amount of

Do You Spend Too Much?

One way to tell if and where you might be overspending is to see how your wage stacks up against this example which finance experts believe is the perfect ratio for money in to money out

25 per cent on housing (rent, service charge, insurance, etc)

22 per cent on food and drink

14 per cent on investments

12 per cent on travel

7 per cent incidentals

5 per cent energy and other bills

5 per cent entertainment

5 per cent on household goods

money you need each month to get by.

Below are some of the most common ways the average person wastes money every single day of the year. If you are that average person, earning an average wage and with average expenditure, simply by changing these few things you could save around £1,000 a year – save that in a high-interest, tax-free account and in ten years you've got about £11,000. There's no catch, there's nothing risky and there's no need for a financial adviser. Each one of these things is probably something you've thought of doing yourself but didn't think it was worth it.

TOP MONEY-SAPPERS

NOT PAYING OFF YOUR CREDIT CARDS

The average person owes about £550 and pays £100 a year interest on this. Borrowing money on credit cards is the most expensive way to get in debt – why do you think it's so easy to get one? Paying off your credit cards should be the absolute first thing you should sort out in the Save Plan – otherwise you're just throwing cash away each month. How do you do it? First switch to a lower-interest card – if everyone in the UK did this, card company RBS Advanta estimate the annual interest bill in the UK would decrease from £2 billion to £800 million. Once you've reduced interest, it's time to start paying off the loan. If you've got spare savings, use those – the amount of interest you're receiving is nowhere near as much as you're paying out. If you don't have any saved cash, your payback plan depends on the size of the debt. Look at the bill. If you realistically cut back elsewhere in your life, could you afford to pay off the minimum plus 20 per cent of the debt every month? If you could, you'd pay the bill off in six months. Don't use the card in this time or, if you have to, ask the company to reduce the limit by the amount you pay off so at least you can't overspend. If the debt's too big to pay off in six months, it's probably going to be better to get a cheap loan, use it to pay off your cards and then cut back to meet the repayments. If you do this, don't run the cards up again. Cut it down to one card (the one with the lowest interest rate) and use it only for emergencies until you're out of trouble.

NOT SHOPPING AROUND

So you just renew your car insurance, your travel insurance, your house insurance, etc. without shopping around because you don't have time. According to the AA, which does an annual comparison of insurance prices, the average customer can save 38 per cent on car insurance (which works out at about £150 on the average premium) and 30 per cent of their contents and building plans (an average of £30–40 per policy) simply by spending about an hour on the phone. I doubt anyone reading this plan earns £180 an hour. With the new internet sites, shopping around is easy, as you can now price things up on-line and find out who is cheapest for you. Try www.screentrade.co.uk. You can also save a fortune on insurance by knowing what

Knowing how you spend can also be a good way of getting spending under control. Here are three money personalities, all of whom have their own personal spending problems – and solutions

THE PAUPER

IT'S YOU IF: You have a lot of money in savings but never any cash. You're afraid of spending money and manage your cash religiously. Chances are you know to the penny how much you're worth, and all your bills are on direct debit. You won't build up your credit card and will probably starve rather than pay interest. Despite this, you worry about money and will often be found doing budgets

YOUR PROBLEM IS: Not your bank balance but your mind–money balance. You don't have any problems with cash so you make your own – this is probably an "inherited" family trait. Instead of worrying about money, you should relax – financially, you're under control

THE OSTRICH

IT'S YOU IF: You don't like the whole money idea. Okay, so you have to have it but you don't want to know about saving and if you get into debt you're more likely to try and forget about it than deal with it. You're the kind of person who doesn't open the letters from their bank manager and you don't really care about maximizing savings or minimizing expenditure because you think that you won't understand. You're actually a bit afraid of all things financial

YOUR PROBLEM IS: Your fear of finance could be costing you money. You're probably paying over the odds on credit cards or for your mortgage and because it seems easier to leave things than deal with the jargon you'll always be worse off than you should be. You need to see a financial expert who doesn't speak in jargon. Don't be afraid to ask for this when you approach a company – if they don't like it, they aren't the right ones for you

THE CASHAHOLIC

IT'S YOU IF: Your credit card is up to its limit, you're always overdrawn – but you don't care. Cashaholics really don't see how much money they have as important – it's what they do with it that counts. They often believe something will turn up to bail them out

YOUR PROBLEM IS: The "something" might never turn up. You spend above your means and while at the moment you don't care, what happens if it all comes crashing down? You're probably wasting a lot of money. Cashaholics should start to scale things back to prevent financial disaster. I know you don't believe this will happen but it's better to have a contingency plan than end up in dire financial straits. Look at both the Save and Splurge plans for help

There are also two sensible money personalities: The realists who if they get into trouble work their way out of it, and the careful spenders who live within their means and maybe have a little debt but nothing to worry about. If you fall into these groups, well done

companies discount for – fitting a smoke alarm, for example, knocks 2–5 per cent off the average contents insurance polic, a car alarm can reduce car insurance by as much as 20 per cent.

NOT ASKING FOR SAVINGS

You went overdrawn by mistake once last year, so why did you pay the fee? Ditto, that credit card payment you didn't get to the bank in time. If you're generally a good customer but you just make a mistake now and then, ask for charges to be refunded – most banks will oblige, saving you 2–3 per cent of your credit card balance or as much as £90 on an unauthorized overdraft fee. Savvy customers will also ask to be excused annual credit card fees (threatening to close your account normally works here), saving £20–50 a year. If they say no and you don't run up interest on your credit card, switch to a card that doesn't charge an annual fee. If you're shopping with cash, you should also ask for a discount. Credit card companies charge stores up to 5 per cent to process a payment – some stores (particularly independents) will waive at least this on a cash payment. You have nothing to lose by asking – and pounds to save if they say yes.

NOT LOOKING AFTER THE PENNIES

How much cash is in your pocket right now? Check again tomorrow and chances are you'll be trying to work out where it went. Studies have shown that the more cash, particularly coins, people carry around, the more they spend – it's like the odd pound or two here and there doesn't count. I know it sounds juvenile, but for one week only, take out as much cash as you plan to spend each day and leave your cashpoint card at home. If at the end of the day there's anything left in your pocket or purse, put it in a jar and don't touch it. The next day, do the same. At the end of the week, subtract what's in the jar from what you drew out of the bank. Then compare the total with how much you normally spend in a week. I asked 20 friends to do this for a week and the savings ranged from 20 to 60 per cent. One serious overspender, Andrew, saved £80 in one week – that's £320 in a month that he's frittering away on impromptu lunches instead of sandwiches, buying takeouts on the way home instead of making do with what's in the fridge and post-work pub visits.

CONVENIENCE

According to Affluenza (a group committed to reducing overspending), the average consumer spends £6 a week on tea and coffee from cafés while at work (lunch is another £15 a day). That's £312 a year on caffeine – is the buzz really that good? Look at where you spend for convenience. Could planning reduce this? Experts say the average family spends £2,000 a year on impulse shopping – most often, on food. Having a shopping list that covers the entire week and sticking to it can dramatically decrease your expenditure. When I first got made redundant, I went to the supermarket every day; when I got my credit card bill, I discovered I had spent £270 on groceries in a month – my normal bill was £80. I also had a freezer full of food I really didn't want to eat. Impulse shopping can be a dangerous thing.

OVERCONSUMPTION

I mentioned a couple of examples of this in the introduction but there are many, many more. We are so used to spending money that we don't think twice about it. Saving the odd 50 pence here and there just doesn't seem worth it – but as I hope you've realized by now, those 50 pences do make a difference. Have a look at some of the following and see how many you could alter in your life.

DO YOU BUY GENERIC PRODUCTS? Many own-brand products are actually made by big-name companies but are sold in supermarkets for up to 50 per cent less. Medication is one area where this is extremely apparent – one leading painkiller, which sells for way over £2 a packet, is exactly the same as its generic equivalent costing 90p.

DO YOU OVERUSE PRODUCTS? We talked about toiletries, but we could also look at condiments, cleaning products, electricity, gas – even food. Ever checked the real serving size on a tub of ice-cream? We buy more goods than we need to and we use them faster. Can you cut back on what you use – and cut back on what you buy?

DO YOU USE COUPONS? The increasing number of supermarket and other loyalty card schemes mean we get sent money-off coupons all the time. Marketing men think a good response to a coupon offer is 2 per cent – the average is 1 per cent. Which means 99 per cent of us are losing out on money. If someone sent you cash you'd use it – why not the coupon? One US consumer, Janet Pare, hit the headlines when she bought $496 (£320) worth of groceries for 3 cents (about 2 pence) by using coupons. You may not need to go that far, but you can save cash with coupons.

ARE YOU BUYING THINGS YOU COULD GET FOR FREE? I saved £100 a year when I realized that I didn't need to take full bottles of shampoo, conditioner, shower gel, etc. on holiday (my mother always does this and so I'd always done it). I started off just decanting things into travel bottles; now I pick up all the soaps and little bottles of shampoo in the hotel room and travel with them. I also bring soap back – I haven't bought a bar in two years! Matchboxes are another unnecessary expense – every time you go to a restaurant, pick a couple up. More and more companies are placing free postcards in restaurants and gyms. One photographer I know uses them almost as business cards, sending one in every time she sends in pictures to a magazine. Look at what's around you for the taking – most companies pay to advertise through these products. They want you to use them, yet most of us think it's cheap to take these things. It's not cheap, it's sensible.

PAYING BY DIRECT DEBIT?
A Gallup survey revealed that 67 per cent of people on budgets failed because of unexpected bills. Your bills also cost you up to 13 per cent less if you pay up-front. Detractors of the scheme say it's a rip-off because the companies get your money before you've used the goods, and yes, if you saved the money you would use to pay your bills in the bank every month it would be a rip-off, but you probably don't. What's more, if you overpay, you get the money back – which is sort of like getting a bonus every April. If you're worried about losing money this way, Direct Debit, the organization that controls the scheme says, "If money is wrongly taken from you, it's up to your bank or building society to refund it immediately. They then must seek recompense from the company that has taken the money. If a company wants to change the amount of your direct debit, they have to give you at least ten working days' notice beforehand."

By now, if you've implemented all the above, you should be on your way to savings of around £1,000 a year, but you could make more. Every year the sensible business looks at its profit and loss statement, to see where it can cut costs. You should do the same. Does your mortgage interest rate need re-evaluating? Are there any discount schemes for bills or in local stores that you could be joining? Every month or so, do an audit of what has gone out of your household expenses and see if you can reduce these without reducing your standard of living.

WHY YOU SHOULD ALSO DO A BUDGET

Now you've plugged the major cash leaks, your money situation will be looking much healthier but why stop there? The amount of money you can gain by altering your lifestyle just slightly is phenomenal – and by doing a budget you can work out where you could save. There are many things that people spend money on without even realizing it. Experts believe that by keeping track of what we are spending we can cut 20 per cent of our expenses without even feeling it. Now, before you roll your eyes, this doesn't mean you have to stick to a restrictive spending programme – for a start, most of the unsuccessful budgets are the ones that don't take into account your actual spending patterns. This budget will let you keep the things you enjoy – and cut back on areas that aren't giving you what you want.

For one month, write down every penny you spend. Include day-to-day expenditure, bills and regular payments, credit card treats, etc. Once you've done this divide your expenditure into sections – exactly how is up to you but good headings to think about are: Household, Work, Travel, Food, Clothes, Entertaining, Treats. How much are you spending on each area? Do you really think that's worth it? Could you cut back – and by cutting back I don't mean cutting these things out of your life completely, just fine-tuning.

We asked 31-year-old personal assistant Sian to carry out this exercise and she discovered exactly how much she was wasting each month. Sian doesn't earn a bad salary – about £20,000 a year, which clears her around £1,250 a month. She spends £400 a month on rent, and £100 on other utility bills, her share of the council tax, etc.; her travelcard costs her £50 a month, leaving her £700 a month. "Yeah, right," says Sian. "I never have that much money – my credit card has £500 on it which really bugs me. Every month I pay £200 off (but then seem to put more on) and I go into my overdraft of £100 every month." We asked Sian to fill in a spending diary for four weeks, including everything from her morning paper to her estimated monthly phone bill.

EATING OUT

Well, that explains £250 of Sian's monthly spend. Sian is forking out a huge amount of money on takeout lunches (an average of £4 a day), croissants and coffee on the way to work (£3 a day), snacks and drinks during the day (£2 a day), takeout food on the way home (£10–15 a week). This is on top of the £100 a month she spends in the supermarket, "on food that tends to go off because I don't eat it". According to average spending patterns, Sian should really only be spending about 5.5 per cent of her wages on food outside the home – she spends 20 per cent. We kept lunch as it is, as Sian said she wouldn't eat homemade sandwiches. However, we did tell her to reassess her accompaniments. Did she really need the 50p bag of crisps and the 60p Coke from the sandwich bar where she bought her sandwiches, or could she bring these in from home (saving about 60p a day)? The main change we made was for her to have breakfast at home (saving £2.50 a day once she's bought her supermarket croissant) and she switched from the coffee bar to the office kettle (saving £2 a day). She avoided takeout for a month and instead bought food at the supermarket that she knew she could cook more easily. "A good rule for busy people like Sian is to only buy food you can make in one pan in ten minutes. You'll only get tempted by faster food options otherwise," says chef Steve Pooley. SAVING: £150

GOING OUT

Another £200 a month went on going out with friends. Sian went out at least one night in the week and went to the pub for a quick drink on at least one other night. She also went out every weekend. This is a lot. According to one study of social lives, the average person spends about three hours a week with friends. Sian doubled that and admitted sometimes she didn't want to go but felt she couldn't let people down. Sometimes a change in attitude is what it takes to save money; a bit of self-esteem chat taught Sian how to say no every now and again (saving about £30 a month). She also readjusted some of her plans. "We always went out for dinner, but instead we started going to the cinema, having pizza at each other's houses, meeting for coffee on Sunday mornings, which reduced the £30 bills to £5 or £10. I didn't feel I'd missed out – and some of the others were thrilled we weren't spending so much." SAVING: £100

CABS

Sian's habitually late and ends up jumping in cabs to get her places on time, thus spending £70 a month. She also often took cabs home in the evening. These ones we left, but the lateness had to stop. SAVING £30.

LOANS

Sian didn't realize how much money she had loaned to her flatmate Becky. In this month, she loaned her £35 and got £15 of it back. The rest occurred when Becky asked her to buy her a Coke when she went to the shop, or to lend her 50p for her bus fare. "Because it's such a little amount I never think about asking for it back, but it really does mount up," says Sian. SAVING: £20

THE REST

Sian's final £200 a month was spent on clothes, magazines, make-up, etc. – little treats she didn't realize she was buying. "I work really near a big shopping mall so it's easy to pop in during my lunchbreak." This was also where Sian's credit card build-up was coming from. Leaving the card at home for a month made a huge difference. She didn't spend anything on it and the £200 stayed off. As she needed the high limit only for paying for holidays (and wasn't expecting to go away soon), Sian asked the company to cut her credit down to £500 – and reduced it further when she paid her £200 off the following month. Once it was clear, she raised it back to £1,000 but only took it on planned (and budgeted) spending sprees, preferring to pay cash instead of run it back up. Her last expense was a £30 a month phone bill and a £35 a month mobile bill – but we decided to let her keep that indulgence.

By doing the above, Sian saved £300 a month and didn't really notice any of it. "It was just nice not to have to think about how I was going to pay off my overdraft or credit card. I know I wasn't much in debt but it did worry me." She's now paid off her credit card and her overdraft, invests £100 every month in a high-interest account (by standing order from her bank account on the day she gets paid, of course) and has started a £50 a month pension fund. Finally, she has an extra £150 cash a month to prevent her building her credit card debt back up.

FOR THE STUBBORN

If, even after I've given you the easy options of cutting back above, you look at your budget and say it's impossible for you to spend less, there's just one more bit of maths to do here. How much do you earn an hour? How many hours do you have to work to afford that part of your life? Now, do you honestly get that much pleasure out of it? Is the coffee from the downstairs coffee bar really worth a week's work? If the answer's yes – we have a problem, you're living outside your means and the Save Plan isn't going to work for you. The only way you're going to get out of your money rut is to make more money – which takes us to the Splurge Plan.

The Splurge Plan (or how to make more money without becoming a workaholic)

The Splurge Plan is for those of you who are tired of working, working, working, but are still not able to afford everything you want in life. In an ideal world, splurgers would win the lottery rather than those dull people who say they won't let the money change them – but we're dealing with reality here, so the cold hard truth is, if you want more money without cutting back, you have to make more money. There are two ways to do this: you can earn money at work or from the bank.

HOW TO EARN MORE WITHOUT WORKING MUCH HARDER

Using up all the time created in the last chapter is not the point of dejunking your money. To earn money without overwork is possible, but you have to be canny.

STEP ONE: ASK FOR IT

Only 22 per cent of people ever ask for a pay rise. Of these, 50 per cent get one. However, the idea is not to just walk into your boss's office and demand more cash. You have to play this carefully. Spell out why you deserve a raise (not why you need one; the fact that you want a bigger house is not your boss's problem). Quantify these reasons, have figures and back-up wherever possible. Have three sums in mind: your ideal, your minimum and something totally out there. Ask for the last one, aim for the first one, and if they won't give you the third, think about walking. One final tip: research by US psychologist Debbie Moskowitz says that Thursday is the best day to ask for a raise. Apparently, bosses are more receptive to new ideas and haven't yet switched off for the weekend.

STEP TWO: SWITCH COMPANIES

You may be getting a pay rise already every year, but that doesn't mean you're going to be that much better off. According to David Opton of career management company Exec U Net, switching companies boosts pay by an average of 10 per cent – and can gain you as much as 20 per cent. However, annual rises tend to be in line with inflation and add up to a paltry 2–3 per cent. "You're never in a better position to get money and perks than when you are negotiating an offer for a new position," says David.

STEP THREE: KNOW YOUR TAX BREAKS

Thirty-six million people in Britain are paying too much tax – much of this comes from people who don't notify the tax office when they change circumstances, so don't pick up any benefits. £650 million comes from self-employed people who aren't claiming expenses, £951 million is collected in fines from people paying tax bills late. Check your tax details and ensure you're on the right tax code for you – your local tax office can give you more information. If you're self-employed, get a good accountant to go through and determine exactly what you can claim back. If you do your own accounts, you may not realize exactly how much better off you could be. And ensure you get the return in on time.

STEP FOUR: READ YOUR CONTRACT

Do you actually know what you're entitled to from your job – and do you claim it all? The obvious thing is overtime payments, which many of us are entitled to but don't feel we can claim. However, there are also things like weekend working allowance, transport costs – even dry cleaning or dress hire if you have to attend black-tie events for the company. Not claiming everything you are entitled to could lose you hundreds if not thousands of pounds a year.

STEP FIVE: ASK FOR MORE PERKS

One of the biggest excuses for not handing out pay rises is that there's not enough in the budget – but maybe there's more to offer you in other budget areas. Is it normal in your position to have a company car? What about stock options or year-end bonuses? If that's too ambitious for your company, how about free gym membership? According to the Institute of Directors, the number of companies offering perks is dramatically increasing – why shouldn't you be in on the deal?

STEP SIX: THINK OF IDEAS THAT'LL SAVE YOUR COMPANY MONEY

In 1991, an American Airlines flight attendant working first-class noticed that the size of caviar tin used would serve the entire cabin but a lost was wasted when the cabin was not full. She put the suggestion to the company that they buy smaller tins so they wouldn't waste so much. Sounds simple? They hadn't thought of it before. Changing to a smaller can saved them over £300,000 a year – the attendant was given a £30,000 bonus! Don't assume your company has thought of everything. Often those in the boardroom don't actually deal with things day-to-day and have no idea of wastage or potential savings.

As Whitney explained, you spend at least one-third of your day at work and around 77 per cent of us admit it stresses us severely, yet still we feel guilty about being adequately compensated for this. You shouldn't. Firms are realizing the pressure workers are under – two-thirds of managers in one recent survey admitted they knew they were putting pressure on their workers but couldn't do anything about it – and they wanted to make amends. If you can be flexible about the level of your demands, you can get results – but you'll never know unless you try.

HOW TO MAKE MORE MONEY FROM INVESTMENTS

You can make money from investments in two ways. You can get risky and carefree with the stockmarket and all those clever unit trust and investment trust things. (If you want to know more about making lots of money or making money fast through investing you need to speak to a financial adviser; see the Resources section of this book.) Instead, the dejunk philosophy for making money through investment is to ensure that every penny you have is working for you. Okay, so you won't make hundreds over night, but you will be richer by the end of the year.

MAKE A SAVINGS GOALS CHART

Generally, saving money is something that occurs at the end of the month if we have anything left over. In our credit-led society it's more normal to go into debt to buy something than save up for it, but this always puts you on the losing end – paying out interest rather than gaining it. You need to know your financial goals. Identify them and identify what it will take for you to reach them. Now start saving. Leaving savings until the end of the month is the sucker's way to save. You won't do it – if you're going to amass money, you have to take it out and put it where you can't get at it before you can spend it on other things. So how do you start saving money without missing it? You could apply the Save Plan techniques and invest the proceeds, but also look for money you won't miss. Since the day he started work, my friend John has invested half of his annual pay rise every month. That was five years ago – he's now saving £150 a month that he never even missed. He uses some of the cash to go on holiday but always retains a minimum balance – at the moment, that's £4,000!

KNOW YOUR INTEREST RATES

The average current account gets about £1.35 interest on every £100 – a year. The average person loses hundreds of pounds a year because they don't put their money into accounts which earn the most interest. It can make a huge amount of difference – say you put £50 a month into a current account paying 0.3 per cent gross – at the end of two years you'll have saved £1,204.60 (£4.60 profit). The same amount saved in a notice account paying 7 per cent will earn you £89 profit. If you save money, check your account interest. Set yourself an "instant access" limit: the amount of cash you want on hand immediately. Everything else should go in a thirty-day or more account. And review your interest rates every now and again – banks do lower them. Just remember most accounts are quoted with a gross interest rate (i.e. before tax is taken off). To find out what you'll actually earn on your savings, multiply the gross rate by 0.8.

STOP PAYING TAX

On most savings accounts you pay tax on the interest you gain – but there are numerous ways to prevent this. Tax-efficient savings plans like ISAs can earn you an extra few per cent on your money – according to research by financial advisers IFA Promotion, not stashing money in these accounts is costing Brits about £1 billion a year. £630 million more is lost where couples investing together don't put savings in the name of the lower taxpayer. How much would using your tax breaks save you? On a £3000 investment held for one year in a tax-free account you'd save £41 a year in interest.

LOOK FOR MISSING MONEY

Eight billion pounds is lying around in bank accounts just waiting to be claimed, say the Unclaimed Assets Register. This includes money from expired life policies, pension funds, national savings bonds and windfalls from conversions. To discover if you're owed anything, write to Unclaimed Assets Register Ltd, 8 Devonshire Square, London EC2M 4PL. "On one of our very first searches we found a insurance policy for someone that was worth £19,000," says Keith Hollander from the register. "The company had been taken over and the gentleman concerned didn't know who by, so couldn't find his money."

GET A MONEY POT

Darren, aged 25, and his girlfriend Lynette, 30, were saving for their first home together. They estimated they'd need a deposit of £8,000. "For two years we had a contingency pot and at the end of every day we threw our spare change in it – normally about £2 a day," says Lynette. "Also, if we gained any money, tenners from the lottery, Christmas presents, etc., it went in it. We also had a trade-off plan. Say we fancied a Chinese takeaway, we had a two-pronged attack. We'd either order one but leave out one dish and put the fiver in the pot – or we'd buy most of it from the supermarket and order the one dish which would make it seem 'real'. This would save us an average of £10 which went in the pot. When I gave up smoking, I put the £2 a day I would have spent on cigarettes in the pot. Two days a week I'd take lunch to work and put the £10 in the pot. If Darren didn't go to the pub on Saturday he'd put the £30 he'd have spent in there. Every month, we'd take all the money out and put it in the bank. At the end of two years we had saved £6,500 and we didn't feel as if we'd missed out on anything."

Knowing where your money is and what it's doing for you can take time, but it can also show results. Never believe your money controls you – you control it and by understanding how to maximize income you can increase your cashflow.

Timesaver Tip: The thirty-minute grocery shop

It's been estimated that every minute you spend in the supermarket after 30 minutes costs you 30p in impulse purchases. So how do you do the food shopping in less time and for less money?

List things. *"Knowing what you want to buy and sticking to it will cut your shopping bill by 20 per cent," says homes and food expert Sarah Lynch. "List what you need for the week – but also things that are running out. The less you can go to the supermarket, the less you will spend. Avoid more than one visit a week or month"*

Only pick the size of carry cart that fits your shopping. *Do not get a trolley if you've only gone in for three items. Carrying a heavy basket is the easiest way to cut short a shopping trip*

Pick the size of store that fits your shop. *If you want a pint of milk, do not go to the supermarket. Go to the little shop where they may charge you 5p more but you're less likely to buy a trolley load. "Also, inner-city 'metro' type stores can save you money simply because the range is not so big," says Sarah. "If you're an impulse shopper there is far less to tempt you and it'll take less time to get round"*

Go on the least busy days and times. *If you're not held up around the aisles you're less likely to pick things up that catch your eye. The busiest days for shopping are just before or after any holiday weekend, Saturday (between 10 and 6; before and after this, the store's deserted), Sunday, evenings between 5.30 and 7.30 and lunchtimes*

Get the mood right. *Most people say never shop when you're hungry, I also say never shop when you're not. If you don't know what you feel like eating later that day, you'll buy four different variations. You also shouldn't shop when you're stressed (well, without a list). You won't get everything you need and you're more likely to buy unhealthy foods. Women should also avoid shopping under the influence of PMS – a study by the Women's Nutritional Advisory Service found 72 per cent of women overspend at this time by amounts ranging from £2 to £175*

Pick the fastest checkout queue.. *Cash-only lines are quickest – and prevent overspending. If you only take enough cash to the supermarket for what you're buying you can't overspend, no matter how long you're in there.*

The Four Financial Life Stages

The final stage of dejunking your money is determining that you have the right long-term financial planning. Having the wrong products is as bad as having none at all. Money can also be wasted if you're getting incorrect information about your financial needs. For example, if you're spending money on life insurance, but have no mortgage or dependants, you're wasting money. We asked a financial consultant to identify exactly what you really need – and how much it should be costing you at each stage of your life. "These are the essentials and they should be started as soon as you can – in your twenties if you're at that stage or right now if you're not," she told us.

THE ESSENTIALS

PENSION

If you're twenty or thirty, retirement may seem a distant prospect, but if you want to retire early then you must think about how to pay for it now. This is particularly important for women who may want/need to take career breaks to have children. If you have an occupational pension scheme – join it. If not, look at taking out some kind of private pension arrangement.

How much should it cost you?

The amount you can put into a pension is regulated and it alters by age – but you should always put in the maximum. If your company pension doesn't take you up to the maximum, you should increase premiums through a supplementary policy called an Additional Voluntary Contribution. Take advice from a financial adviser as to which type is best for you.

In your twenties: You can pay 15 per cent of your salary into a company pension, 17.5 per cent into a private scheme

In your thirties: You pay15 per cent in a company scheme, 20 per cent into a private pension scheme

In your forties: You pay 15 per cent in a company scheme, 25 per cent into a private pension scheme

In your fifties: 30–35 per cent of your income should be going into your pension.

SAVINGS

You should get into the saving habit as early as you can in your working life. Completely essential, whatever your age, is to try and build up three months of outgoings in an easily accessed account in case of emergencies (possibly with 30- days' notice, which will pay a little more interest if you don't need your money). If you have any spare cash, you should also think about longer-term savings, schemes tying up your money for five years or more with exposure to the stock market. Take advice on the most appropriate vehicle for you – and don't forget that investments can go down as well as up (we have to tell you that, it's the law).

How much should it cost you?

In your twenties: The ideal situation now is to be putting 10 per cent of your net salary into savings – this is the time when your financial responsibilities are likely to be least so you should maximize this now.

In your thirties and forties: Residual savings for investment may be sparse but you should maintain your emergency fund.

In your fifties: You may want to think about buying a final five- to ten-year plan to maximize the money you have after retirement.

INSURANCE

Some kind of insurance is vital, whatever your time of life – but you should ensure you have the right kind for your needs.

How much should it cost you?

In your twenties: You need life insurance only if you have dependants and/or a mortgage. You should, however, look at earnings protection that will pay you an income if illness prevents you from working.

In your thirties and forties: You will probably have dependants or a mortgage by now, so life insurance is important. If you have children you should be looking at a policy that pays at least 10x your income for every two children. You should also have critical illness cover. If you have children you might also want to think about medical insurance.

In your fifties: A policy for long-term care is important. The Community Care Act passed responsibility for long-term care to those requiring it, not the state. One in three people will eventually need help with carrying out their normal activities. If you have any estate (pension, property, savings, income, etc.) worth £16,000 or more, you must pay. The average amount of care needed is for four to six years at an average cost of £25,000. Forty thousand homes each year disappear to pay for long-term care. Cover should offer £1,000 a day – £2,000 is better.

After the above are in place, you can start looking into other areas of investment. See a financial adviser who can look at your priorities, and, if you have reached your thirties or forties without a pension or savings, can advise you how to make up any shortfall. It doesn't matter if they are linked to a company or independent. What's important is that they can look after you long-term and that you feel comfortable with them. If you don't understand financial jargon, go to someone who doesn't speak it.

Summary

We need to concentrate on our attitudes to money rather than on the amount we have. Once we understand that what we have is not who we are, dejunking our finances becomes much easier

Knowing exactly what you are worth is the key to long-term financial freedom. Most of us have a dream and if many of us reassessed and redistributed our assets, we could live it now

Most of us waste hundreds of pounds a year. By changing seven simple areas of their life, the average person could save £1,000 – and there are many more

Knowing exactly where your money goes each month can cut spending by 20 per cent

We have to learn that it's okay to be compensated for the work we do. Half the people who ask for a pay rise get one.

Making sure any money in banks/building societies works for you maximizes income and can help develop your investment strategy. Studies from Barclays Bank show that people who are in tune with their savings have better-planned and more profitable schemes than those who don't look at what goes where each month

Having the wrong financial investments is as bad as having none at all. You have to tailor your long-term planning to your life stage

Action Plan

Work out how much you own and owe to determine how much financial freedom you actually have. If the news is not good, start a plan to determine how to change things

Do a cash drip audit – where can you plug the cash drain in your home?

Write a budget for one month. What gives you pleasure? What could you do without? Start looking constructively at where your money goes each month. One month, follow the cash-only plan and see how much you save

Do some research at work. Are you paid the correct rate for your skills? Does your package reflect the others around you? If not, what will it take to improve things?

Look at all your investments. Are they working hardest for you? The weekend papers and money sections of the weekly papers do round-ups of the cheapest credit cards/mortgages and the highest-earning accounts. Would you be better moving your money? Also look at your long-term financial future – are you covered in terms of pension, insurance and savings? If not, what would it take to put that in motion? Start today – once you have a savings account, watching it build up can be addictive!

Chapter 6
Dejunk Your Work

AS WE'VE DISCUSSED, we are now working longer hours than ever before, we're under more stress and more financial pressure than ever before – and at the heart of all these drains on our minds and emotions is work. Fifty-four per cent of people in a world-wide study by the Associates for Research into the Science of Enjoyment (ARISE) said work is the main cause of stress in their lives. One in three office workers would not pick the same career again. Seventy-seven per cent of working women would quit work if they could.

Why Do We Need to Dejunk Our Work?

The reasons for our dissatisfaction are many. Part of it is that our minds haven't yet caught up with society. It's now the norm in the UK and the US for both parents in a family to be working, yet the cultural ideal is that only one parent should work and the other should stay at home with the children. When work hinders our family role, we have problems; when family hinders the work role, we have problems. This work/family meshing is an intrinsic part of modern life yet we have not come to terms with it, causing guilt and pressure which affect every element of our lives. "Getting the balance between home and work organized is one of the most important quality of life factors for people today," says Professor Cary Cooper, occupational psychologist at the University of Manchester Institute of Science and Technology.

Work is no longer as pleasant as it used to be. Whereas it used to be seen as a sociable place to make friends, many psychologists now believe insecurity and low job satisfaction are spoiling interpersonal employment relationships – a recent study by ARISE found that increasing numbers of young workers dislike their colleagues. Working in a hostile or negative environment is draining on the emotions and on motivation.

Our working hours are also a problem. We spend at least a third of our day in a working environment – and more and more of us are extending that time, willingly or otherwise. It's therefore no surprise it's stressing us out. "The work ethic of companies has changed over the last decade or so. We are told to work longer, to work harder and that if we don't our job is at risk," says Cary Cooper. "The speed we are expected to work now is phenomenal – e-mails, faxes and mobile phones all demand immediate replies and we just work faster and faster but for longer and longer." This goes against our personal work ethic that determines that we want to spend more time at home, with our families or on ourselves. Cooper calls it presenteeism: "Being at work when you should be at home ill or relaxing with your family." Yet even when we are given time off we don't want to take it. Sixty per cent of us don't take vacations because we don't think we have time and a recent study from the TUC found that six out of seven people entitled to parental leave won't take it for fear of it looking unprofessional on their job record. The long hours culture is firmly engrained in our psyche. We cannot accept the idea that we give to our job and that it should therefore give back to us. This conflict is causing major problems in our working and personal lives.

IT'S AFFECTING OUR HEALTH

"More people than ever are drinking or smoking to excess," says Cary Cooper. "We are less likely to exercise because we're too busy and the stress we are constantly under is suppressing our immune systems. The current work situation is making us sick." In fact, 43 per cent of women studied by *Top Sante* magazine recently admitted to having taken up to six days off work a year to escape their feelings of overwork. An ARISE study found that this trend is worldwide (and most prevalent in Hong Kong and the US) and across all levels of professions. Some companies are even offering mental health days for staff to refresh their cognitive batteries.

IT'S AFFECTING OUR MINDS

As well as stress to contend with, the power struggles in today's working environment are also affecting the way we think. Studies have shown that the suicide rate for men is 3.7 times more than for women and it's believed that the power swap that has occurred in the working environment has contributed to this. Just recently, companies like HSBC and Mazda announced they are offering gender-affirming counselling for men depressed and disillusioned by the mixed sex competition in which they now work.

IT ALTERS YOUR BEHAVIOUR

"People are increasingly finding that work is overlapping with their personal life," says Cooper. "You start to notice that you're more irritable, more aggressive and that you've lost your sense of humour. This can affect your relationships with partners, family and colleagues." The *Top Sante* survey also discovered that 55 per cent of women shout at their children because of pressure they are under at work.

IT ACTUALLY AFFECTS WHAT YOU DO

"Someone who has downshifted their life is more effective than someone stuck in the nine to nine nightmare," says Cooper. "Lack of support, fear of job loss and lack of control all take their toll on what you can actually achieve. An organization that runs under the millennium work ethos of fear is not going to achieve any more than its more caring competitors. One study I conducted revealed that a quarter of chief executives don't enjoy their work because they can't spend time with their family – unhappy workers do not make for a happy company."

How Do You Dejunk Your Working Life?

Well, the answer is not necessarily to give it all up. "Most people who are dissatisfied with work believe that this is what would make them truly happy," says career consultant Jo Ouston. "It's not always the case. Most people who think they hate working are actually only dissatisfied with one element of their working life. It may be the hours they work, the company they work for, it may be the job they are doing or the people they are doing it around, and only once you determine exactly what you want from your working life will you know how to fix it." You also need to know what you want from work – do you want a thrusting career or just a job that pays enough for you to spend time with people you care about? Do you thrive on a reasonable level of stress and hassle or is the millennial, work faster, work harder, work ethos not for you? Knowing what's wrong with a job and what you want from a job are the factors that are going to help you get the balance right and you can do it, whatever your career. A few years ago, Washington was shocked when 52-year-old Bill Galston walked out of his job in the Department for Domestic Policy with no apparent warning. He'd only been there eighteen months and was on the fast-track to political success. The gossips came up with many scandalous stories, but the truth was that a few months earlier Galston had received a letter from his nine-year-old son detailing all his achievements for the last year that Galston had missed. It ended with the line, "Baseball's no fun when there's no one to applaud you." Galston chose to change his career to spend more time with his family. He was helping run a country and one would assume he had the salary to prove it, yet he quit – so what was your excuse again?

HOW TO IDENTIFY WHAT'S WRONG

The key to dejunking your working life is finding out what's wrong with it in the first place – Jo Ouston recommends the following exercise. "It really helps you find out what's right for you," she explains. "And that might be completely different from what you are expecting."

1 THINK OF THREE JOBS

Think of the best job you've ever had (doesn't matter how long ago or whether you could make a living from it now). Using the same criteria, identify your worst-ever job and then think of a friend's job that you would really, really like.

2 IDENTIFY CHARACTERISTICS THAT TWO JOBS SHARE BUT THE OTHER LACKS

For example, two of them may involve working long hours, two of them may offer the chance to deal with people every day – don't look at these positively or negatively, just identify at least twenty characteristics that the jobs share.

3 NOW PUT THEM INTO TWO COLUMNS: POSITIVE AND NEGATIVE TRAITS

You can now start making comparisons between your current job and what you want and don't want from a job. Obviously the more positive attributes your current job has, the less of a problem you have to solve it. Look carefully at the negative attributes: are these things that you can change without fundamentally altering your job or employment structure, or will you have to change role, company or even your entire career?

The good news is, there has never been a better time to dejunk your working life. Companies are rapidly realizing the effects the work ethic are having on employees and are looking into more viable ways to deal with this. What's more, society is changing to make taking control of your working life more acceptable. Changing hours, taking breaks or altering the path of your career are no longer seen as abnormal. "The idea that you have a job for life is no longer the only working ideal," says Jo Ouston. "This gives us great power when it comes to making the break." People are also beginning to realize that change doesn't have to be for ever. Employers are coming to terms with flexibility and so are employees. The absence of the jobs-for-life culture means we can begin to explore the idea that work can be dynamic. That we can

How Do You Get Your Boss to Agree to Your Dejunk?

Now you've determined how you'd like to change your working conditions, how do you get your company to agree?

KNOW WHO TO ASK. Some companies have established policies regarding flexible working, in which case you need to determine who to approach – there's no point getting the agreement from your line manager if this is a company-wide issue

PLAN, PLAN, PLAN. "You should try and work out what you want and how long for. It could be that you want the situation to occur permanently, just during school holidays or while you care for a sick relative or some other temporary situation that's putting pressure on your time. You should also have some constructive ideas on how to implement the scheme; how you would handle things like emergencies or client contact; and what you would see as the situation regarding payment. If at all possible, you should also have back-up from other people in similar fields that shows the idea can work," advises Charlie Monkcom

have fast and slow periods and that when we make a break it doesn't have to be for ever, which opens up a whole range of opportunities for us as individuals. In the next few pages we'll look at some of the solutions available to help you decide – and you do have to decide. And you need take some time over it. "People spend more time planning their vacation than thinking about what they want to do with their lives," says Atlanta-based career coach Bill McDonald, in career magazine *Fast Company*.

Solution 1: Dejunking Your Hours

Time and time again in this book we've pinpointed the time crunch we are all experiencing. Working fewer hours is top of the wish list of almost 80 per cent of workers, yet most of us believe we can't actually achieve it. You can. Sometimes it's simply a matter of altering your way of working and if you're happy in your job and with your position, then the time-management chapter of this book should solve your problems. But if you decide that to dejunk your work truly you need actually to alter the hours you work, there are a wealth of opportunities open to you. Companies are steadily beginning to realize that a static nine-to-five culture is not always the best way to get work done. Around the world the possibilities of reducing our working hours are becoming established. France has a 35-hour working week; Belgian labour laws offer mothers up to three years' parental leave; in Sweden, flexible working hours worked out on a monthly minimum and maximum limit are commonplace. So what options are open to you? Dejunking your hours can take three main forms: you can adapt your way of working to be more productive so you get more done in less time (see chapter 4 on time management). You can reduce the number of paid hours that you work, or you can adapt the physical structure of your work so that although you may not be reducing hours or pay, you can be happier with the balance.

REDUCING YOUR PAID HOURS

Thirty per cent of people would like to work less than thirty hours a week – most say they don't for financial reasons. However, you may not be as badly off as you thought you would be. Working full-time is expensive. What with travel, clothing, food and childcare, the average worker spends around £3,000 a year on actively going to work and that doesn't include expensive holidays to de-stress, impulse purchases at lunchtime and after-work drinks. By reducing the hours you work you can reduce some of these expenses, which can make the whole thing more viable. To work out how likely this is for you, total up how much you earn in a year – include your monthly wages after tax, an average amount of overtime payments, bonuses and any benefits that you would have to pay for if you left (like free medical insurance). Now calculate how much you would save if you cut your hours down – think what you'd save on travel, childcare, lunch, etc. Look at whether you'll be paying less tax by reducing your wages. Subtract savings from wages – how does that compare with what you'd earn if you went part-time? If you think you could do it – but aren't sure – give it a try now. Calculate how much you'd earn if you did cut down on your paid hours and live on it for three months. If you can just about manage while you're still in full-time work, you'll definitely manage when you cut down your time and expenses. By doing it you'll know, and by saving the excess cash you'll have a small nest egg to keep you feeling a little more secure.

If the news is good news, you now need to look at the options that are open to you. The most obvious is part-time working.

PART-TIME WORKING

Part-time working is defined as working fewer than 30 hours a week. Gone are the days when part-time work meant low pay, low skills and no benefits. Recent legislation has led to more job security and benefits for part-time workers and as such it's becoming a viable working proposition for many workers – some particularly forward-thinking companies are even allowing senior-level positions to go part-time. "Companies are realizing that part-time workers are often more motivated and have more energy," says Charlie Monkcom, co-ordinator of New Ways To Work. "The numbers of people working part time now adds up to one quarter of the population and we are expecting this growth to continue in the future." Just be careful. Without some personal planning, you may not gain all the time you were hoping for – particularly if you're female. Research has revealed that women working part-time have just one hour more free time a day than full-time workers. Use time-management controls to ensure you don't fill your new-found time with tasks.

JOB-SHARING

Like part-time working, job-sharing was once seen as something that could only be applied to low-responsibility positions but many new high-profile appointments have meant that charities, the medical profession, journalism, the legal profession and retailing are all now using job-share to its full potential. The idea is that the normal working hours, pay and benefits of a job are shared equally or pro-rata between two employees. Tim and Deirdre are husband and wife solicitors who job-share. Tim works Monday, Wednesday and Thursday; Deirdre works Tuesday and Friday – they have a full-time shared secretary. "We took the decision to do this at the time our daughter was born," explains Tim. "I was working full-time for a firm of solicitors and wanted to leave. When Katie was born I took six weeks 'paternity leave'. That was when we hit upon the idea of doing a job-share. We decided we could bring the children up ourselves rather than hiring a childminder. Deirdre met a mutual acquaintance who was a partner in a solicitor's firm – his first response was that it wouldn't work but we persuaded them and it does work. Working three days a week is wonderful. I spend more days at home than I do at work. The job is still stressful and there are times when you still have to meet deadlines but you just have to be more organized. I can't leave the work till the next day because I won't be there. The downside is that we are operating on one salary. If we both worked full-time and hired someone to look after the children we'd be miles better off, but I see my children more and that's something I would never have been able to do working five days a week."

V-TIME

American readers will be far more *au fait* with the concept of V-time than the British, as this concept has been established there since around 1976. The idea of V-time is that you trade income for time off. You can reduce the amount of full-time hours that you work by 5–50 per cent for a specified period of time – a year, six months, whatever, and your wages are adjusted accordingly. In a culture where companies are looking for ways to cut costs without cutting productivity, V-time is proving a very viable budgeting exercise and many experts believe that we'll see more of it in the future.

TERM-TIME WORKING

New Ways to Work define term-time working as "allowing employees to remain on a permanent full or part-time contract but giving the right to unpaid leave of absence during the school holidays. These total about thirteen weeks a year and the average leave entitlement is between four and six weeks. There remain about seven to nine weeks of possible unpaid leave." It's obviously the way that the education profession has been working for years but very slowly the idea is creeping into other areas of employment: 4.3 per cent of employees in the UK now work on a term-time basis. When voluntary organizations officer Shaheer's wife died, the strain of looking after his six-year-old daughter began to show. "I was taking more and more time off and during one consultation we came across the term-time scheme another council ran. I worked out the hours and the money and discovered that by not having to employ a childminder during the holidays I was actually better off. Now I have the whole of the summer holidays off and all yearly holidays like Christmas and Easter. My wages are averaged out throughout the year, so I receive an income even on those months when I'm not actually going into work. It doesn't really affect my job – people are used to companies having people away on holiday in the summer."

Changing the Way Your Hours Are Spent

Trends predictors believe that staggered working hours are the future for society. Some experts believe that more companies will adopt the new flexible working procedures so that actually working nine to five will no longer be the norm. Others predict that we will start to work in two shifts; one shift starting early in the morning and finishing early afternoon, the other starting at lunchtime and finishing early evening. Some researchers even suggest we'll work day-to-day shifts, spreading a 35- or 40-hour week over three or four days. Which will work best remains to be seen. You can incorporate some of the benefits of "shift" working into your life now with some of the new working patterns.

FLEXITIME

While you're still committed to a set number of hours a week, flexitime allows you to work when you want to and spread your time commitments accordingly. If you want to take your children to school in the morning, you go in later. If you want to be there when they get home, you go in earlier and leave early. If you want to take a day off but don't want to use your holiday, you can work extra hours. Flexitime is possibly the best established of the new working conditions in the UK today, with many local authorities adopting the policy. Andre works for Hammersmith and Fulham Council in London. "I'm contracted to work a 37-hour week and can come and go when I like. However, the main benefit of flexitime for me is that it lets me accrue hours that I can take off in lieu. This means that most weeks I work over the 37 hours, normally coming in around 10 and leaving at 7. This earns me a day off every three or four weeks. That time's important to me. My weekends are busy with tasks or social engagements yet these days off can be just for me. Few people are around so no one need see me. I do think it makes me a better worker – and if I had children it would definitely improve my life with my kids. If I moved companies I don't know if I'd go to a company that didn't offer flexitime – they'd have to offer me a good package to replace it."

ANNUAL HOURS

Again, this is a scheme more commonly used in the US than the UK. The idea is that you are contracted to a company to work a certain number of hours a year. In some companies this is run like flexitime – it's up to you how and when this occurs – in others it's scheduled around peaks and troughs. Again, this makes valid economic sense – why have employees around when you're not busy and have to employ casual labour at peak periods? Expect to see more annual hours contracts soon.

Solution 2: Changing Where You Work

Much of the dissatisfaction of workers in the current climate comes from where people are choosing to work. This can be for two reasons. First, it's simply a matter of environment and convenience. Commuting takes hours out of every week and switching some or all of your work to a home or local environment can reduce much of the time crunch. The other problem with the working environment comes down to atmospheric dissatisfaction – where the people, politics or even wallpaper of your workplace are getting you down. We'll deal with this first.

WHEN YOU HATE YOUR COMPANY AND YOUR COLLEAGUES

Internal organization conflict is on the rise. A study by ARISE revealed that 29 per cent of office workers have no confidence in their company's management, 32 per cent feel unappreciated at work and 7 per cent hate their physical surroundings. "The companies we are working for are making us more insecure and more likely to dislike authority and those around us," says Cary Cooper. "We feel as if we have little control and that spills over into the other areas of our lives." Sixty-two per cent of employees say their organization has undergone some kind of restructuring in the last year. It could be new technology or new working objectives, but whatever it is, it's breeding insecurity in workplaces across the world – 46 per cent of American workers are worried about their jobs and feel under pressure to prove their value.

The answer here is simple. You like your job and you don't mind the hours that come with it; instead, your dissatisfaction occurs because of those around you. Your solution is to find a similar job in another company. In the UK, on the day I write this, there are around 300,000 jobs available. So how do you maximize your chances of finding and getting the one that you want?

1 USE YOUR CONTACTS
By asking someone to refer you to an employer, you'll get noticed, recommended and probably be employed. Referrals generate 80 per cent better results than cold calls. Most people you meet have 250 contacts you could get in touch with – anyone you ever want to meet is just four or five other people away. You just need to pluck up the courage to approach that initial contact.

2 DON'T ALWAYS WAIT FOR AN AD
If there is a company you would like to work for, write to them. Make your letter original, don't make it look as if you're just sending out a circular to every company. There's no job there yet so you have to make it look as if you really want to work for this company – and that they really need you.

3 HOW TO REPLY TO AN AD

Tailor your letter and CV to include as much information about the job and the company as you can. Remember the rules of the perfect CV – it should be one page; it should only use positive words, it should mention only assets relevant to that particular job and as many of them as are truthful. If a stack of applications come in for a job, the average person sorting through spends about twenty seconds scanning your life's work – you don't want to get dumped because they can't be bothered to read to page two to discover that you do speak fluent French.

4 IF YOU GET AN INTERVIEW, GO PREPARED

Know your way round the company and the industry. Make every answer you give show another of your skills and reveal what you can offer to the job. If relevant, take a package to leave them, containing your CV and any relevant cuttings from trade papers about you, references and ideas for which they have asked. Put as much work into the interview as you would into the job.

5 ONCE YOU'VE ACED THE INTERVIEW

Send a thank-you note. "It helps you stand out – and gives the opportunity to say anything you didn't get across in the interview," says management consultant Mary Horsnell.

WHEN YOU HATE WORKING FROM THE OFFICE

If you like your job, but don't like the company politics, the commute, or the person who sits next to you, the obvious solution is to work, at least some of the time, from home.

Telecommuting, as it's known, is one of the fastest growing areas in the working world today. Henley Management College has revealed that 36 per cent of companies are now using teleworkers and that by the year 2004 this is expected to rise to 70 per cent. UK Home Office statistics claim that one million people now work from home at least one day a week – in the USA, the number is closer to six million. In either country these people are a mix of the self-employed or, increasingly, they are people whose companies have realized the benefits of lowered overheads and the increased productivity of home-working. Heather works for NatWest Group in their technological department. She works nineteen hours a week and goes into the office once or twice a fortnight. "I started working like this at a time when a lot of people in the office were having children and the managers were concerned about keeping staff – this seemed a good way of doing it. I think it works well, but I do find I need motivating. My motivation is my children. Whenever my concentration is wavering I think if I don't get my work done now I'm going to have less time with them. That's enough focus to keep my concentration on the work. Working from home saves me three hours travel each day. The flexibility allows me to fit in with young children's lives yet still fulfil my need for a career." Sixty per cent of office workers would like Heather's life, but could you be one of them?

SO ARE YOU READY TO WORK FROM HOME?

There are many benefits to working from home. You're less likely to get sick because of reduced stress and reduced exposure to colleague-spread germs. You'll get up to 30 per cent more work done – and you can feel smug about helping the environment (a BT report believes that if just 15 per cent of the workforce became teleworkers, we'd cut around half a billion gallons of pollution). You'll also save money, time and stress – if you do it correctly. "When we listen to telecommuters whose work styles and personalities are good fits with telecommuting, we hear the most wonderful stories about how they have regained their sanity and a sense of balance and control in their lives," says telecommuting expert Gil Gordon. "But when we listen to those who for one reason or another began working from home against their better judgement we hear just the opposite." Home-working isn't always the easy option; you can end up working longer hours and feeling even more dissatisfied than before. So what are the pitfalls you should be looking out for?

Do you have the right personality and resources? Gil Gordon recommends you ask the following questions. Do I have the self-motivation and self-discipline to work at home? Do I have suitable space to allocate for a home-office area? Have I made realistic arrangements for my children? Can I stay away from the refrigerator and other temptations? Can I get by without constant contact with others?

PROCRASTINATION

Not having anyone else around you can make it difficult to get started in the morning. Setting a morning routine can really help here. "I start work when the postman arrives," says politics researcher Anna. "Occasionally I might get something done before then but normally I'm just pottering about tidying my desk, reading e-mails and making coffee, but when the post arrives, I go to the office, close the door, open the post and get started."

COLLEAGUE ANIMOSITY

You know you're working, your boss knows you're working – how do the poor wheelrats back in the office know? Home-workers can often experience bad feeling from those left behind. "As a society we are accustomed to associating 'work' with the office and relaxation with being at home, so the natural tendency is to somehow assume that telecommuters aren't really busy," says Gil Gordon. "You have several options to change their views. First, make sure that your co-workers are aware of what you are producing. Don't take too much credit for your work or otherwise act like a superstar, but make sure your work doesn't become invisible. Your manager may be able to help you stay in the limelight in this respect. Second, be sure you use the phone, e-mail, fax and whatever methods available to stay in touch with your co-workers while you are away. Third, consider inviting one or more co-workers to visit you in your home office. Once they see you aren't lounging on the sofa or working in the bath (you aren't, are you?) and they see that you actually have a functioning office at home, they'll probably start acting differently."

INTERRUPTIONS

Children, family members and neighbours all find it quite acceptable to drop in to see you when you work from home. You need to develop signs and signals that show you're not available. This can be particularly hard for children to understand, so you may need to make them visual – or even wearable. If you stay behind a locked door all day you'll go mad, but if coming out means mum or dad are available for play, things could get tricky. Wearing a "work" baseball hat means you can come out for coffee without ending up playing with Lego for half an hour (don't worry, you don't need to wear it at your desk when you go back into the office).

OVERWORKING

While you may be working from home in order to work fewer hours, you may find you spend more time at your desk. Commuting time can easily be taken up into typing time and it can be hard to switch off when the office is just a few steps away from the bedroom. Other people can also fail to respect the boundaries and call at hours that they wouldn't have been able to reach you normally. The best solution for this is to install a separate phone line, but if you can't afford it, or don't want to change your number, take the advice of Robert, one home-worker who prints his working hours on his business card. "It's decreased the amount of late-night calls by about 90 per cent," he explains. "If anyone else calls out of hours I tell them I'm just flying out, so could I note down what they need and call them back in the morning?"

ISOLATION

Working from home can be lonely – especially if you decide to make it your permanent base. It's can also be harder to bounce ideas off people and not having that easy second opinion can be difficult. "About four of my friends work from home and we're all in creative fields," says Amanda, a journalist. "We have a brainstorm morning once a week. We check by e-mail who can make it (there will always be at least two of us) and we go for coffee. We discuss our problems, read each other's ideas or work we're not sure about and swap gossip. It's great for security and it ensures you're not too out of the loop."

CAREER ADVANCEMENT

It can be a case of out of sight, out of mind when it comes to promotion for home-workers. If you are interested in career advancement it is important to keep visible within the organization and make those that matter aware of your achievements. Gil Gordon says that managers should help you with this. "Most line managers of telecommuters report that they are more promotable because of the experience of working at a distance. It demonstrates their capacity for responsibility."

Solution 3: Getting the Power Back

Increasingly we are losing power in the working environment and this leads to many problems. Many studies have revealed that it's those workers who feel they have the least control over their jobs who experience the most stress and the most dissatisfaction in their working lives. But how do you get the control back?

START TO ENJOY THINGS

This is one of the most important ways to take back control at work. By making yourself enjoy your job, you get through each day faster – but also create a positive vibe that can help you move on to better things. If you're depressed and fed up it will show in your work, your attitude and also any new applications you make. Focus on what you like about your job or, if you really hate everything about it, set yourself targets or goals to entertain you and keep you focused. Jez works for a telephone banking service in their call centre; he enjoys it, but some days it can get really dull. "On those days I make up stories in my head about where people got the money they are dealing with – and what they're going to do with it. My favourite was the day someone I knew was only 22 by their records transferred £30,000 into their account – I could have written a film script that night."

WORK ON WHAT YOU CAN CONTROL

The truth is, even the most senior people in a company come up against things they can't control – but they are probably happier if they don't dwell on them. Use this approach yourself, forget worrying about things that are beyond your control. Do them, get them out of the way, and focus on what you enjoy and can control.

CHALLENGE YOURSELF OUTSIDE THE WORKING ENVIRONMENT

Marketing-executive-turned-yoga-teacher Elaine believes training for a cycle ride across Cuba gave her the confidence to take the leap into an unknown career. Leading US CEO Candice Carpenter told *Fast Company* magazine, "My character was formed by mountaineering. Enduring rainy slopes and cold bivouacs to spend an hour at the top of the world shaped my ability to handle adversity. If you're not afraid of the hard times, obstacles become utterly unimportant." As you'll discover in more depth when you reach the "Mind" section of this book, many psychologists believe that how we think about things reflects what we get out of them. If you start challenging yourself outside the working environment, you'll be more likely to develop and overcome challenges in your working environment.

LOOK AT WHAT YOU WANT FROM YOUR JOB AND FOCUS ON GETTING IT
Your job has two parts. There are the outside trappings – the title, the office, the pay, the benefits and the perks – and there is what you get from it, your day-to-day tasks. You need to decide which of these is most important in your life and focus on regaining control and finding happiness in that.

GO FOR PROMOTION
Trying to move up in your existing company is a great way to change the power balance, but if you're not ready you can feel even more out of control. Career consultants recommend asking yourself the following four questions before you make the move for promotion:

• Are you confident in your abilities?
• Do others think you are good at your job?
• Are you always willing to help out during times of crisis?
• Can you cope with new demands?

Then consider how good you are at: delegating; dealing with disputes; coming up with new ideas; and problem-solving.

If you don't want to move up, don't be afraid to move sideways – or even back. Sometimes moving up is not right for you or the path your career is supposed to take. We get hung up on the idea that our career must progress upwards, with more money, more underlings and more prestige, but this doesn't always mean more of a challenge, which is the most important thing in any job. You have to be stretched in what you are doing, or titles and remuneration just don't matter. In fact, the new zig-zag career path is fast becoming the new model.

WHAT ABOUT STARTING UP ON YOUR OWN?
Working for yourself can be one of the most rewarding changes you can make in your working life, but with 65 per cent of new businesses failing in their first five years you have to get things right. Your local bank, citizen's advice bureau and the internet are loaded with advice on how to start up and the ins and outs of financing, patenting and so on. If you like the sound of being your own boss, you should use

these resources to check out how to go about it. Look at the following to determine if it's a realistic idea.

1 HAVE YOU GOT A VIABLE IDEA?

Is it needed and cost effective? Does it have a consumer base and do you know how to reach it? Have you got the cash? Have you got the self-starting personality, the enthusiasm and the million and one other ideas that need to be brought out at a moment's notice when things go wrong? Having the right personality is as important as the idea when it comes to setting up on your own.

2 DO YOU REALLY NEED TO SET UP ON YOUR OWN, OR CAN YOU JUMP IN WITH SOMEONE ELSE?

Buying into an existing business, taking over one that's being sold or investing in a franchise are ways of being your own boss that don't necessarily entail so much risk.

3 HAVE YOU DONE YOUR RESEARCH?

Do you really know what this involves? Have you sourced suppliers, storage, transport, etc? Look at everything physical and all the mental and specialist skills your business is going to need and find out where you are going to get them from. If you can't get them, then don't get started.

4 CAN YOU SIDESTEP INTO YOUR BUSINESS?

Quitting a secure job to start your own business is risky – and will leave you with regret if it all goes wrong. Is there any way you can soften the blow? For most companies, this means starting off as a sort of moonlighting exercise alongside your full-time job (or at least taking a part-time job to ensure the bills are paid). When 36-year-old marketing executive Elaine quit her job, she knew she wanted to teach yoga but she also knew it would take a long time before that paid the bills – so she set up her own travel marketing company to work in part-time. "I got the control and self-satisfaction that I needed, but I didn't take that much of a risk," she explained. You should also look at any career break options your company offers.

A 1991 survey from *Personnel Today* magazine discovered that 12 per cent of organizations offered career breaks. These are normally given unpaid, with the intention that at some point in the future the employee will return to work, but they could be the break you need to turn your life around. Ex-police officer Justine used one such break to start her new life. She'd been fed up for a while, but then one final incident, when she was assaulted, convinced her. She decided to take a two-year career break (the force allowed breaks of up to five years).

She took a job selling cosmetics for the Virgin Cosmetics Company and began building a team of women who wanted to work with her. She now runs a team of 240 and has a turnover that runs into hundreds of thousands. "This job is everything the police wasn't," she explains. "I had the chance to take control of my own life and my own diary. I love working from home and deciding where, when and how I work. I know that all my hard work and long hours are for my benefit. I have the opportunity to write my own pay cheque and set my own goals.

"Within a few months of starting I had a small team that has since developed into one of the most successful in the country. I found that I was really good at it, that I had found my niche in life. I have just won three national awards to prove it, the recognition and support is just fantastic. I actually get rewarded for doing something I love. Previously I was only 'told off' for things I'd done wrong. I am now really happy, confident and financially independent. It was the best decision I have ever made, and I made it thanks to the career break. Knowing in the back of my mind that I could go back to the police force was a huge cushion, it gave me the confidence to try something new – and that changed my life."

Solution 4: Change What You Do Completely

Would you describe what you do as a job, a career or a vocation? You may think that the three are the same, but that's not true. Each of these words may refer to your employment, but which you choose to describe how you spend your working day speaks volumes about how you feel – and what you should do next.

IF YOU SAID JOB . . .

Chances are you're not happy. A job is often seen as something transitory and a way to pass the time and earn the money to live rather than something that can actively give you pleasure. It's perfectly acceptable to have "a job" if you're happy in it – but if you've already decided that you're not doing what you want to do, this is a sign that it's definitely time to get out.

IF YOU SAID CAREER . . .

Many of us believe that this is what we should be aiming for. Careers say success, they say prestige, they say cash and they say that you're motivated – they don't say that you're necessarily happy. Careers are those things which make us work long hours for no pleasure. Ask yourself what it is about your career that makes you happy. It could be something as simple as the five minutes on a Monday morning when you brief your team. Look at how you can expand that in your current role – or exploit it in a new working environment.

IF YOU SAID VOCATION...

You don't need to change what you do. All of us should be aiming to work in our vocation. A vocation is defined as "a calling" – what you are meant to do with your life. It's something that gives you pleasure – and that has some kind of impact on those around you. It doesn't have to mean finding the cure for cancer. Have you seen that schmaltzy advert for the gas company where the cherry-cheeked young man helps the pensioner get his heating working? If the emotions in that advert are real, that man has found his vocation. This is what all of us should be aiming for. Whether you're working in something creative or manual, you should be able to adapt your daily duties to fulfil the vocation criteria.

Obviously it's not always as simple as that. The average worker changes tack three times in their working life – and it can happen at any point. There are many possible reasons for it.

IT WASN'T WHAT YOU SHOULD HAVE DONE IN THE FIRST PLACE. Very often we choose careers because they are what we are good at – not what we enjoy. Greg was excellent at maths at school. Throughout his life everyone had told him he should work in finance. He became an accountant – he hated every minute of it – because he didn't know what else he'd be "good at". After five company changes in as many years, he started working in the accounts department of a music booking agency. "One day there was a crisis with a client who was refusing to pay a band on a job and I was the only person the band could get hold of. I sorted things out and enjoyed it. Over the next few months I got more and more involved with the talent side – I'd offer to answer their phones when they were at lunch or while they were busy. I started booking people into jobs I thought they'd be good at. I managed to organize difficult schedules and negotiate better fees. I learnt that attention to detail and dealing with difficult creditors had taught me loads about organization and dealing with people – as soon as an opening came in that department, I took it."

THE JOB CHANGES. Tracey had worked in a bank since school. She loved it, she loved dealing with people and personal contact, but then the banking world changed. It became paper-driven and goals-focused. Personal care went out of the window in return for meeting targets and maximizing profits. "I hated it. I was doing the same job, with the same people, but it wasn't right for me any more," she explains. "When I got the chance to take redundancy, I jumped at it. Now I work in a care home, paying out patients' allowances and balancing the books. There's no pressure and I really feel I'm helping people."

YOU CHANGE. When Steven was 21, running a night-club was all he wanted to do. When he got to 34, it was tiring and frankly quite ridiculous. "I was in the suburbs. I was no Peter Stringfellow and I felt silly. I didn't love the music any more even though I'd sunk my entire life and money into this place. I wanted to work during the daytime again. It wasn't viable for me to sell up so I hired a manager and left him to it. I check the takings and that's that. The rest of the time, I'm a rep for a brewery. My contacts at the club got me the job and I enjoy it. I'm still meeting people, still feel like I'm in entertainment, but I don't feel old any more."

UNFORESEEN CIRCUMSTANCES. Joanne always wanted to be an undertaker – even at school: "Everyone thought I was mad." At sixteen she began training to become one of the UK's only female embalmers. "But then one morning I woke up and I couldn't see properly. My vision was blurred and I could hardly open my eyes. After much investigation, we discovered I had developed an infection that was set off by the embalming fluid. I was told that if I didn't stop I'd damage my sight. It was a crux moment for me – I didn't know what to do next, I'd worked too hard to go back. So I decided to quit completely. I messed around for a while and then decided to train as a paramedic. It was hard work, I had never really studied at school and although this was on-the-job training I still had to learn a lot and fast. People think it's funny that one minute I'm dealing with dead people and the next I'm trying to save them, but the skills are the same. You have to be able to walk into a room, assess the situation and take control. You have to deal with people who are very distressed and try and make them understand what's happening. The only real difference is you can drive an ambulance a bit faster than a funeral car."

Change can happen to all of us at any time in our life. It can occur in three ways. You can change your job but remain in the same field. Let's say you're a finance director of a hospital, you could switch to personnel in that hospital. You can change field but keep your job title – becoming finance director of a record company, for example. Or you can change both, quitting the finance and heading off to make organic cheese.

Of the three, the last is the hardest change to implement. In fact, our cheese-making finance director probably wouldn't have had that many problems. "To find employment we truly love, we should be looking at what gives us a buzz in life," says Jo Ouston. "You need to analyse what in your life makes you truly happy and find out how you can use that – but you also need to take into account the skills you have. The big reason people fail in their new ventures is that it's just too far removed from their normal realm of experience." Assuming our finance director was a cheese lover, he'd have been fine, as the success of his venture depended on many of the skills he'd have learnt in his previous jobs. If, however, he'd decided to go off and be a doctor, he could have had problems. "It's rare that anyone jumps from one career to something totally unrelated," says Jo Ouston. "Normally there are some skills in common, it's more adaptation of what you have already learnt but used in a different area."

What Next?

MAKING THE CHANGE

STEP 1

Determine what you want to do. You need to look at which parts of your job and which parts of your life give you the buzz Jo was talking about. Can you combine these to make a career? Say your three skills were writing, investigating and dealing with people, and the three things that gave you most pleasure were animals, music and travel. You could look at careers in specialist journalism or PR; a protectorate position like welfare for the RSPCA or complaints for a travel company; brochure writing for travel companies; something in music publishing. Many, many areas are open to you by mixing up those skills

STEP 2

Work out why your past career went wrong – and ensure you're not going to come up with the same problems in your new one. If you had problems with sales targets and stress, you probably need to move away from any kind of competitive arena for a while – don't forget that no change is ever permanent, you can always come back

STEP 3

What type of company do you want to work for? Large, small, established, new? You've determined that what's most important to you in a job are the inner layers, the self-fulfilment and sense of achievement that you get from finding your vocation in life – but are the outer layers equally as important to you? If so, you're probably looking for a large, established company which pays more and offers more benefits.

STEP 4

Just who are you going to work for? Do you want your own level of control, perhaps by working for yourself as a temp, or your own company, or do you enjoy the stability a larger company can bring? Knowing which you'd prefer helps you ensure you're getting what's right for you and narrows down your selection criteria

STEP 5

Get out there and get started. This is the hardest step. You need to work out what it is that's going to make the change possible. Do you need more qualifications, more experience, more money or even more chutzpah? When Chloe got fed up working as an admin assistant in an chocolate company she decided to work in retail as a salesperson for a fashion manufacturer. She had no retail experience, but she researched the accessories market, went to trade shows, checked out what was selling and who was hiring. When she saw an advertisement for a job with a well-known accessories firm, she faxed a CV, letter and references. The letter told them exactly what she thought would sell next year and why. She enclosed suppliers' details that she thought she could bring to the company (people she had met at shows and a few she had never even met) and she signed off by saying if they didn't take her now they would only have to headhunt her in a few years. With no experience, she landed an interview and the job. It was her knowledge that did it – her lack of qualifications didn't even get noticed. She took that first step and didn't look back – and is now reaping the rewards with a high salary and the respect of her peers.

QUITTING WORK COMPLETELY

Sometimes this is the right choice for you – particularly if you have young children. If you firmly believe that quitting work will solve more problems than it creates, then you should go for it. For more information on making a major change like this, read chapter 11, "The Total Dejunk". And good luck.

What Areas are Going to Grow in the Next Ten Years?

If you want to make a success in a new career or start a new business, it's important to tap into where the growth areas are going to be. So where should you be looking for work?

PERSONAL SHOPPING/PLANNING/ADVICE

Trends predictor Irene Wilson believes people are no longer going to have time to make choices and purchases for themselves. She feels we'll take on life managers in the same way as we have financial or bank managers to organize everything from our career to our wardrobe. It's already starting to happen.

HOME SECURITY

Faith Popcorn believes we're going to want to make out homes safer and security is going to become paramount in our minds – she calls it "armoured cocooning". Research reveals the thing young people are most afraid of is the increase in crime and so getting into the protection business could pay off.

HEALTH AND PERSONAL CARE

Labour statistics say this area has been growing for the last five or so years and it's not expected to stop. As the baby boomers get older and our population lives longer, more health care is going to be needed than ever before.

THE NURTURING PROFESSIONS
Work trends predictor Carole Pemberton believes that these types of careers will make up almost 80 per cent of vacancies over the next five years.

THE INTERNET
The number of shopping outlets on the web has increased tenfold in the last year. The internet is now responsible for the second highest number of employment placements. And it's growing.

How to Write a Change of Career CV

If you're swapping fields, it can be hard to work out exactly what you should put on that bit of paper that sells you to those who count. You don't have the experience they are looking for, so why should they hire you? Well, are you so sure you don't have the skills? "Many of us get hooked up on the idea of formal qualifications and doing tasks in an office environment," says Mary Horsnell. "Just look at those women who return to work after having children and say they have done nothing for the last five or six years. They forget to mention running a home, supervising school trips, being vice-chairman of the PTA, treasurer of the residents' association, etc. All these require skills, you just need to know how to sell them." So what are the rules for the CV?

- **Find out what the job needs. You only ever need mention relevant skills on a CV, so don't worry that you can't do shorthand if the job doesn't need it. Sounds obvious, but many people get hung up on stuff like this.**

- **How many of those skills do you have – and can you quantify? If the job requires people management, how often have you organized staff? It doesn't have to be a major part of your job description, you just have to do it**

- **How can you beef up your qualifications? If the job requires word-processing skills and you don't know one end of a keyboard from another, you do have a problem – but it's easily fixed. Many colleges have one-day courses. Book yourself into one and put it on the CV – by the time you get the interview you'll know your way round a computing package**

Summary

Work is the cause of most of the stress in our lives. By getting what we want from work we can get what we want from most of our life

Many of us believe that it would make us happy to give up work entirely. This is only true for a tiny percentage. Instead, the problems we have with work are more likely to lie in areas like the hours we work, the location of our work, the power we have or our day-to-day activities and goals

Finding out which of these causes you problems is the key to dejunking your work

It's never been easier to change what you want from work. Society is changing and the jobs-for-life culture is over. You should exploit it

Action Plan

Find out what you really want from your working life and what you don't like

Work through the relevant section

Then check out the other sections to see if they can add to the changes you have made

Reassess your career every year (pay-rise time is a good idea). Are you getting what you want? Should you move on? Should you change some smaller elements? It's easy for all of us to stagnate and we are afraid to make changes in case the time is not right. You'll never know if the time is right until you make that first break

Chapter 7
Dejunk Your Stress Levels

WELCOME TO THE DE-STRESS ZONE. *If time overload is the epidemic of the modern world, then stress is the plague. Its symptoms range from minor ailments like headache or back and stomach pains and progress up to major conditions like heart attacks and potentially even cancer. A 1999 study by a US life insurance company found that 40 per cent of people thought their job stressful and that 39 per cent of those were thinking of quitting because of it. Stress manifests itself in prematurely ended careers, broken relationships and shattered lives, yet it's something that most of us are happy to put our bodies through, day in, day out. One of the most important ways you can dejunk your life is to eliminate much of the stress from within.*

Of course, some amount of stress is good. "We need some level of pressure to motivate ourselves to do things; without some adrenaline, we might not get up in the morning," says Hampshire-based stress consultant and registered hypnotherapist Carole Allen. "But prolonged stress can only damage the body." The reason is that stress puts you into a state of arousal – hormones are released that cause your muscles to tense, your pupils to dilate, your mouth to dry up and perspiration to start. All these things get you ready to run or fight whatever it is you're up against. Unlike our caveman forefathers who were regularly faced with sudden danger, most of the stresses in our lives aren't something we need to run and fight, they are ongoing pressures that we need to learn to tackle. What this means is that our stress system is switched on but the processes that signal it to switch off never actually take place. We spend our lives consistently in some degree of hyped-up state. The level of stress it therefore takes to push us over the edge is much less and the next thing you know, you're irritable, tearful, depressed, tired or worse.

What Determines Our Reactions to Stress?

We don't all experience stress in the same way. It takes an awful lot to push some people over the edge but others will fret over the tiniest amount of extra work. Many factors come into play here. Personality is extremely important; if you have an anxious, ambitious or perfectionist personality, you are more likely to experience stress easily. Introverted people tend to have a higher stress threshold than extroverts who'll find themselves flying off the handle at the slightest opportunity. Your upbringing is also relevant. "One of the first things I ask when someone comes in to see me with a stress problem is what their family was like," says Carole Allen. "People whose parents dealt with adversity calmly and clearly are less likely to overreact to moderate stressors". New research suggests that gender may be important. A study undertaken by Canadian researchers found that while both men and women experienced raised blood pressure at work, when men got home this effect disappeared. The blood pressure of women stayed high – probably because of all they had to do in the domestic environment. Finally, stress can actually become addictive. We start to enjoy the buzz it gives us and can't actually function without it.

And How Do We Overcome It?

The first thing you need to do is deal with what's causing your stress. The triggers for overload are many. Almost anything negative can trigger a stress reaction in a susceptible person. The first step is to work out your most common stressors and how to deal with them. Most of the common causes of stress – lack of time, too much work, difficult relationships – are dealt with in far more detail throughout the rest of the book. If you've gone to the index and turned straight to this chapter (hey, I don't blame you, you're stressed and you want it sorted), take five minutes to try and work out what causes your stress. Is it having too much to do? Is it family problems? Is it that you're disorganized? Identify the two areas of your life that cause you the most stress and turn to those chapters to work on them. Otherwise it's like your doctor giving you painkillers when you know you've got a slipped disk: you'll be up and running for a day or so but then you're flat out for six weeks. Spend time dejunking what's causing your long-term, 24–7 stressload. Once you've done that, it'll be easier to tackle stress when it hits – especially if you use the damage limitation plan that follows.

Stress can affect practically every part of our body and mind. Take a look through the following symptoms; the more you suffer from, the more stressed you are likely to be.

MENTAL SYMPTOMS

Insomnia, racing thoughts, extreme worry, introversion, extreme extroversion, irritability. Basically, any unusual change in behaviour or extreme of behaviour can be attributed to a stress reaction.

PHYSICAL SYMPTOMS

Hair loss, dry skin, headaches, neckache and backache, teeth-grinding, clumsiness (and related bruising), tightness in the chest, breathing difficulties, sweating, stomach or digestive conditions like irritable bowel or knotting in the stomach, itching, tingling in hands and feet.

STEP 1: PREPARE FOR STRESS

While sudden stresses like a death in the family come out of the blue, there are many stresses we can prepare for. Christmas is one of the most stressful times of the year, yet every year we go into it blind. If you know there is likely to be a busy period coming up at work or socially, prepare for it. You might find that some unexplained stressors actually occur in patterns and have clear triggers. Thirty-six-year-old finance manager Mary had a monthly meeting she hated and, while she knew she got so wound up in the few days before it, she didn't understand what was causing her problems at other times of the month. However, after completing a stress diary she realized that her other monthly stress attack occurred the week before this meeting – when the agenda arrived. On these days she fluffed projects, snapped at her partner and felt dreadful. "Once I realized this, I began to plan round it. I'd try and finish big projects before agenda day, I'd make sure I was eating well and go to the gym. I did the same in the days before the meeting itself. It worked; while I still hate it, I'm less likely to go over the edge when some little thing goes wrong." Knowing your triggers and working out how to act against them is vital to tackle stress. To determine yours you need to keep a stress diary. For a month, note when you feel really stressed and when you feel really relaxed and note what's going on around those times.

STEP 2: KEEP YOUR AROUSAL LEVEL LOW

Stress is like a house of cards, it gets higher and higher and suddenly one tiny playing card sends the whole thing crashing down. When you're going through a period of stress you need to keep the amount of cards you're piling up as low as possible. What this means is not overloading your diet with stimulants like caffeine, giving yourself plenty of time to get from A to B so you're not freaking about the vagaries of public transport, and so on. But also check your environment. Constant noise can be stressful; if you're too hot you increase arousal; even the flickering of flourescent lights can send you a few notches up the stress ladder. Do everything you can to keep your arousal levels low so you don't go into the danger zone.

STEP 3: WRITE LISTS

This works in two ways. Writing down what you're worried about can help you prioritize what you can deal with so you can get it out of your head. What's left should be subjected to a perception audit. Write down everything that's stressing you. Then think what the worst thing that could happen to you is (sickness, redundancy, your children being kidnapped, use your own trigger). Now think of the likely consequence of what will happen if you don't do what you're stressing over. Compare every item on your stress list to your worst-case scenario list on a scale of one to ten. If it's under a six, forget it: just concentrate on tackling the big stuff.

Relaxation is one of the most powerful ways to keep stress at bay. Whether you indulge in formal meditation or simply sit in silence for a little while each day, stilling your mind can have a profound effect in calming your body. Once you're practised at de-stressing, you can do it anywhere – but it can be extremely beneficial to have somewhere that you devote completely to relaxation. Soon, just entering this place will start to calm your nerves, slow your heartbeat and reduce tension in your body. US author Shira Block once told me, "It's like the jitters you get when you go to the dentist, just more positive."

SOLITUDE: Twenty minutes spent alone can be more rejuvenating and therapeutic than an hour of leisure time spent in the company of others

NOISE: Noise increases heart rate, disturbs sleep and leaves us in a state of permanent arousal. The modern-day form of relaxation is usually permanent stimuli from the flashing lights and constant noise of the television but what this means to our bodies is that they are never completely switched off. Silence helps you think and it helps your body repair itself. The perfect sanctuary is quiet – if not silent

LIGHT: Relaxation is so much more powerful in the dark. Just sitting with your eyes closed for a few minutes is enough to still your mind and slow your heartbeat. If you're out and about and need to relax, try palming

SMELL: The power of scents to calm has been established for many years and using aromatherapy oil in your de-stress zone can increase your ability to calm yourself. The most relaxing oils include lavender, ylang-ylang and neroli

STEP 4: USE CALMERS

Keep some stressless stuff around. Instant calmers include lavender oil, Bach flower rescue remedy, valerian or camomile teas. Quite often, just the action of using one of these is enough to lower your arousal level so that you can get things under control. If you can follow all these steps when you do find yourself getting pressured at work, around the holidays or just when things are getting you down, you'll find you'll be able to deal with your stress in a more calm, controlled manner – and it won't overwhelm you. However, you also need to work on ensuring you keep stress levels low generally. Taking regular time out during the day and taking a break at weekends can help here, but it is vital to take time out for vacations.

The Importance of Holidays

According to Dr Michael Argyle in his book *The Social Psychology of Leisure*, 74 per cent of people working full-time in the UK are entitled to paid holiday – yet only 60 per cent of those people actually take their holidays. This can have a number of effects. A study published in *Psychology Today* in 1980 found that people who took holidays were less tired and irritable, less worried and less likely to suffer from physical problems like headaches than those who didn't. A study by Boots the Chemists discovered that industry is losing millions of pounds a year from tired and stressed workers who just won't take a break.

By not taking a few days out of the office environment we miss a valuable chance to recharge our batteries. "There are two main reasons why busy people don't take holidays," says Carole Allen. "Fear of discovering the truth about others' abilities – or discovering the truth about their own. People who suffer the first emotion are afraid to let go of the office because of what they believe won't happen if they're not there. They either don't trust their staff or are not confident enough with delegating to risk leaving someone else in charge. The second reason applies to people afraid of what will happen if they leave the office. They think that all of a sudden people will realize they can run the place when they aren't there and that they aren't indispensable after all. This can be hard for people to handle – particularly if they have low self-esteem." Finally, in our culture of long working hours it can almost seem like slacking to take time off for holidays and many people experience extreme guilt and stress prior to going on holiday – it's almost as if by saying we need a week off we are saying we don't care. "People believe it shows how in control and dedicated they are," says Carole Allen. "But that just reflects our after-hours culture. In Sweden, for example, if you work overtime every night and don't take your holidays you're seen as inefficient and are less likely to be given respect."

Knowing when you're stressed and dealing with it as it's happening is very important and there are as many methods as there are people. I listen for something I call the swoosh. I discovered this when I was having real trouble sleeping. Put in some foam earplugs and lie down on your back. Start to slow your breathing and listen to your heartbeat. As you get used to your heartbeat, you'll start to hear the different sounds of the blood pumping round your body – at some point you will start to hear something that sounds like swoosh. Don't ask me what it is, probably some valve moving around. But once you manage to hear that and listen for a minute or two you are so relaxed nothing can faze you. Knowing that this was my instant calmer, I decided to check out a few friends to see what they did

"I know when I'm stressed because I start to feel as if I can't take a breath properly. So I sit for a few minutes and concentrate on breathing in and out – it always works." Alison, 51, nurse

"I play Tetris on my computer. It's mindless and I can just concentrate on that for ten minutes – and if I win I feel I can take on anyone." Billy, 42, graphic designer

"I light a candle and stare at it for a minute or two – my mum always told me to look for the centre of the flame but of course you can never see it. I find it incredibly hypnotic." Jennifer, 45, travel agent

"Whenever I find myself losing it, I pinch the end of my little finger – it just brings me back down to earth and stops me saying things I'd probably regret a few minutes later." Mark, 32, IT manager

"I go to boxercise class. Not only do I get a workout, it's incredibly satisfying being able to hit something – it's not really something women do that often." Rebecca, 29, teacher

HOW TO HAVE A STRESS-FREE VACATION

Anyone who has ever stayed in the office till 10 p.m. writing lists of what should be done while they're away and has been on the phone at the airport gate adding things to that list will know that sometimes going on holiday can be extremely stressful. A survey by Atlanta-based careers firm The Highlands Project once found that 50 per cent of high earners contacted their office at least once while they were on holiday – so how can you ensure that your time out of the office really is time off?

- **Clear everything you can before you go.**

- **Leave a list of all unfinished business with colleagues. Delegate absolute responsibility to them and make sure everyone knows they're the person in control. When you return, don't change everything they did. First, it'll sap your colleagues' confidence; second, people will resent you for going away.**

- **Leave a message on your voicemail to ensure that people know you are out of the office and whom they should contact in an emergency.**

- **Don't tell anyone who is likely to panic where you are going. If you feel you should leave a phone number, leave it with a colleague you trust to try and solve things without calling you for advice.**

- **Don't take any work with you. If it's not there, you can't do it. If it's there you probably won't do it but it'll haunt you incessantly.**

- **Days off can be the most stressful of all vacations as you never quite get away from your work – and people are more likely to disturb you. If you're going to have a day off make it either a Friday or a Monday – research from the University of Sheffield shows these are the most relaxing days, partly because they allow you to switch off and not keep thinking "I must do that tomorrow" and partly because it normally takes a day to unwind from work pressure. If you have to have a day off in the week, turn your answerphone on and do not take calls from the office. One day really isn't going to cause the downfall of the company.**

Timesaver Tip: The one-minute de-stress

"During stress many people hold tension in their shoulders," says osteopath Mike Evans. *"By decreasing that tension you can instantly calm your body. Sitting in your chair, relax your shoulder area and drop your shoulders down. Concentrate on your breathing and push your hands towards the floor. You should feel the stretch at the back of your shoulders. Hold for 30 to 40 seconds."*

Summary

Stress is epidemic in society today – up to 80 per cent of visits to doctors are believed to be linked to the problem

How we react to stress depends on inherent personality and learned factors but also exactly how much low-lying pressure we are under

Finding and tackling the source of day-to-day irritations can reduce the effects of stress

Stress often comes in predictable cycles and you can protect against it

Most of us who are due holiday don't take it all. We should. Taking a break can reduce many of the physical and mental symptoms of stress

Action Plan

Determine what causes your reaction to stress. Can you do anything about it? Will changing your behaviour reduce the stress you are under – are you sabotaging yourself with unrealistic deadlines, etc.?

Find your most common stressors and deal with them

Plan for the other stressors and start building your body's defences against them

Take holidays

Chapter 8
Dejunk Your Mind

THE WAY WE THINK affects every element of our life – even if we don't realize it. The problem is many of us fall into negative thinking patterns that hold us back. Thirty-three per cent of people feel guilty much of the time; 25 per cent of the population suffer medical problems linked to anxiety and worry and 37 per cent of us are permanently affected by low self-esteem. Dejunking helps you reassess normal thought patterns and make the most of what life offers you.

When we're born we have a pretty positive frame of mind. We like ourselves, we don't know what we can or can't do, we don't feel guilt and we don't screw ourselves up with negative thoughts. In fact, until the age of about three the mind of a small child is in a pretty stable emotional state. The problems begin once we start growing up and develop the ability to make the most of this neurological nirvana and also start to learn the emotional bad habits that hold us back.

Remember the well-known quote, "You can't be happy with the world around you if you're not happy with the world within you." That's never been more true than now. Our lives are full of external pressures yet exactly how these affect us is completely our decision. We can perceive anything positively or negatively – and which we choose generally follows a pattern governed by an internal belief system developed over many years. Most of us don't realize this. "And very few people realize the control it has over us," says US therapist Tony Schirtzinger. "Our beliefs work like an 'internal compass' that influences almost everything in our lives and definitely everything that is important to us. Areas like career, relationship choices, how you react to stress and to opportunities that life presents are all governed by this subconscious thought pattern."

In the late 1960s a clinical psychologist called Dr Albert Ellis developed something called the model of human emotional disturbance, also known as the A,B,C system, which attempted to explore this pattern. Its premise was that we don't go through hard times because of actual events that happen in our lives, but because of the incorrect and negative ways that we react to them. He believed that if we could change these patterns of thinking we could react to even the most difficult events in a more positive way. Applying the ABCs to your life is the key to dejunking your mind. In the model, A stands for the activating event that you react to; B is the belief that determines how you react; and C is the emotional consequence of that outcome. For example, say your partner left you (the event). You may believe they did this because you are a bad person who can't hold down a relationship. The consequence of this is that you become wary of forming another relationship, the ones you do form you begin to hold back on and negative relationships become an increasing spiral in your life. But what would happen if you had had a different belief, if you believed your partner had left because they couldn't cope with your recent promotion, either they were threatened by your success or resented not being the centre of attention? The consequence here could be that you determine there's nothing wrong with you but with the type of person with whom you form relationships. For your next partner you choose someone career-motivated or independent and your personal life moves forward positively.

Okay, so it's a simple example but it's a realistic one and it proves that it only takes a change in the way you view something to change your entire future. Dejunking your mind really is the final step to dejunking your life. For some people it will merely be the icing on the cake, the final touch that ensures everything you've worked on up until now falls into place. For others it's more fundamental. Whichever group you fall into you have nothing to lose. So how does your belief system work? Take a while to apply the ABCs to the major decisions you've made in your life. What was the real reason you made those choices? Can you see a pattern emerging? For the next few weeks or months, look at your actions and thoughts and see what's behind your choices. Does it confirm that pattern? As you do this you'll come to one of two conclusions. The first is that you're thinking positively and that you actually have a well-developed internal belief system. "Although all internal belief systems are unnecessarily limiting, some do work well," says Tony Schirtzinger. "What's more, we all eventually gain control over *some* of our unconscious beliefs as we mature, so it's possible that you will have worked on the areas that were affecting you negatively." The second, more likely, option is that you can identify some negative feelings that affect what you do in all areas of your life – and that these are preventing you making choices that will move you on. "Updating this negative internal belief system helps you develop more control over your life," says Tony. This isn't as hard as it sounds. Chances are, at the root of your negative beliefs are one or more of the following: low self-confidence, guilt, worry, negative thinking or suppressed emotions. These are the five negative thought patterns that psychologists believe affect most of our lives.

Low Self-confidence

Low self-confidence is a combination of a reduced faith in your abilities and a dislike of some part of your physical or psychological make-up. It manifests itself in many different ways – introversion, poor body image, shyness, procrastination, personal relationship difficulties. If you're prone to low self-confidence you'll be unlikely to push yourself forward, find it hard to take a compliment and may even be prone to violent or abusive relationships (or merely seek out those where you're the underdog). Low self-confidence can occur in just one area of your life – your career or your looks, for example – or it can span across all the areas. Wherever it hits it can have negative effects; your looks, work, friendships, even day-to-day encounters with authority figures can all be affected negatively by low self-esteem. It can even affect your health. US research has revealed that people who blame themselves when things go wrong suffer more illness than those with a more positive mental attitude.

WHY DO WE LOSE OUR SELF-CONFIDENCE?

Self-confidence is a trait that we're born with. We have confidence in our abilities and we like the people we are. Just look at children when you give them something new to try: they have no fear of consequences, no fear of rejection or embarrassment, they just give it a go. However, as we get older this natural self-belief begins to be chipped away. Experts believe that before the age of eighteen we have been praised 25,000 times (mostly before we reach the age of three) but we have been put down 225,000 times. It's therefore no wonder that we begin to lose any feelings of self-worth that we may have. The negative elements are all around us.

OUR PARENTS

Comments made by our parents are some of the most fundamental determinants of our future confidence. We see our parents as role models and throughout our lives many of us unconsciously live by their views and their opinions.

OUR PEERS

Childhood bullying, childhood attitudes and childhood roles are all vital determinants in how our self-image grows up. Take Ruth. At the age of 33, Ruth weighed 18 stone. She wanted to do something about it but couldn't exercise. Why? Because at school she was the one who dropped the ball, who fell off the ropes, who was picked last for the rounders team. She didn't believe she could ever be good at any kind of sport. In desperation, she started walking (going out at 6 a.m. so no one would see her). Six months later, she started to jog slowly – within a year she had done a three-mile run and over two years she lost 6 stone. "I realized that now I couldn't do team sports or co-ordinated activities but it didn't mean I couldn't compete against myself. Now I'm training for another three-mile run that I want to do in under 25 minutes. Beating that confidence barrier has changed my life, physically, and emotionally I'm far more prepared to take risks now." Even once we mature, the actions and words of those around us can sap our confidence. Negative colleagues or bosses can destroy the confidence of even the most extroverted adult.

YOUR CULTURAL UPBRINGING

People in "emotional" countries like the Caribbean and Latin America have a better self-image than those of us in "cold" countries like the UK or Scandinavia. The reason is believed to be that it's common in emotional countries to offer a lot of positive reinforcement. Cultural speech patterns can also help us develop confidence. In Britain, for example, we are told that statements like "I want" or "I need" are rude and we're conditioned to say the more subservient "May I?" or "Could I?" In the US, however, "want" and "need" are natural ways of expressing desire.

LIFE EVENTS

Major events like bullying, child abuse or poor parental relationships are particular factors in low self-confidence.

OUTSIDE INFLUENCES

Media images are incredibly powerful in determining how we should look or behave. They reveal our images of success and failure and, if you don't conform, can destroy feelings of self-worth. A recent study comparing women in America with women in Iran (where westernized media images of perfect, half-naked bodies are banned) found the Iranian women had a better self-image than did their US peers. But it's not just bodies – it's how much you should earn, acceptable job patterns and the possessions we should have. If you don't conform to what others believe is your lot in life, it can destroy feelings of self-worth. In fact, successful people can develop even lower self-confidence if they don't quite make the grade. Studies at Cornell and Northwestern Universities found that students who nearly reached a higher grade felt worse about their results than those who just scraped through with a lower grade. We always concern ourselves with what we should have done rather than concentrating on the success of what we have achieved.

Confident Body, Confident Mind

If you appear confident to others, they'll treat you as such. This creates a positive confidence cycle and allows your self-esteem and sense of self-worth to grow. So what signs say "treat me well"?

BEING WELL DRESSED. The better dressed someone is, the more confident people expect them to be

DON'T CLENCH ARMS OR HUNCH UP. Bunched or closed postures signify insecurity

MAKE EYE CONTACT AND SMILE. Both say you're happy with the situation and yourself

DON'T LEAN YOUR WEIGHT ON ONE LEG. It says (literally) that you're a pushover – you should also stand with your toes pointed outwards

LOWER YOUR VOICE. Lower-pitched voices are viewed as more authoritative than squeakers

SO HOW CAN YOU BOLSTER YOUR SELF-CONFIDENCE?

Well, it's not simply a matter of looking in the mirror and telling yourself you're happy with your lot. "You're not," says counsellor Genevieve Blais. "Why would suddenly telling yourself that you are change things?" Instead you have to work through a series of steps that help you identify why you lost confidence in the first place – and then try and reverse this pattern of negative thinking. This can take some time, so you shouldn't expect to change things overnight, but they can be changed and the more you learn to like yourself and develop confidence the more your confidence will grow. "The first step here is often the hardest, but it's the one that's most vital to take," says Genevieve.

FIND THE TRIGGER

As we said before, many factors can attack self-confidence and finding and tackling the areas that affect you are the keys to rebuilding your negative self-image and learning to like yourself again. One of the easiest ways to do this is to write a confidence diary. Write down all the events in your life that have affected your confidence negatively; even if you can't remember them exactly, try to remember details like roughly how old you were, what happened and who was there.

NOW ANALYZE THOSE EVENTS

If it was a comment that led to your negativity, ask yourself how true that comment is to you now. Should it really be affecting your life? Look at this realistically and objectively – it can help to ask the advice of others who know you well and will be honest with you. "A huge esteem-basher for people is how they feel about their body," says psychologist Deanne Jade. "Two out of every five women and one-third of men are unhappy with their overall appearance. Of people who are of average weight, 47 per cent of women and 29 per cent of men think they are overweight. In many cases the trigger was something that was said to them in the past. Once you can get them to see that that image is not true, that the comment is no longer relevant to them, if it ever was, they can start to move on." If what it is that is making your feel bad about yourself can be traced to an event in your life (a parent leaving, for example), try and work out why that affects you now and how true the belief you put on to yourself actually is. Many children of divorced parents do believe the divorce was their fault and this can affect many of their life choices.

DEVELOP REALISTIC GOALS

Often our lack of confidence comes from not living up to an imagined ideal – yet that ideal can be far beyond our actual abilities. Without a realistic goal, you will never match up to what you believe you should be and will therefore always feel low in self-esteem. If you are aiming for something and find yourself disheartened because you haven't achieved it, look at what you are trying to do. Is it actually realistic? If it is, look at why you're not there yet and deal with what's stopping you. If you decide the goal is unrealistic, reassess your aim. Look at where it has come from and check you are trying to please yourself and not others (a huge reason for people overreaching). If you are doing something solely for you, try to formulate a realistic version of your goal and write down how you are going to achieve it. Take small steps and put them in motion.

STOP ALL NEGATIVE THINKING ABOUT YOURSELF

If you catch yourself thinking "I can't" or "I shouldn't", assess if that's true. Any negative thinking can promote feelings of insecurity. Earlier, Genevieve Blais said that affirmations alone won't work. That's true, but, combined with other steps, positive phrases can speed the healing process. Think of a sentence that expresses what you are trying to achieve and keep repeating it to yourself. Don't use negative phrases when you affirm – the brain doesn't understand negative phrasing. If you tell it "You're not going to get nervous when you stand up to do that talk", all your brain will hear is "You're going to get nervous when you do that talk".

AND START THINKING ABOUT THE POSITIVE

We can't all be confident about everything – we need to remember that we all have our strengths and weaknesses and we need to emphasize the first and work on the second. Studies from Northwestern University, Illinois, found that the more roles a woman has, the better she feels about herself. The reason given was that these women felt they always

Five-minute Psych Tip: Create a "Want To" List

Very often we sap our own confidence by putting pressure on ourselves to do things we really don't want to do – or which are beyond our range of capabilities. One way to stop this is to write a "want to" list. The first step is to write a list of all the things you think you should do in the next week, month, year – whatever time frame works for you. Write on all of them. "In the next week (or whatever) I should ..." Now go through the list and look at why you should – no, not because you have to, but the real reason – because your partner would like you to lose 3 stone, because the kids won't do their own ironing. For anything that isn't a definite "must do" emergency that's going to save the house from fire or yourself from bankruptcy, go back and rewrite the list prefixing every "task" with "If I wanted to I could ..."

Now look at that list. Look at what YOU really want to do for YOU

had something good in their lives. If their work was going badly, they could concentrate on their positive role as wife or friend. We can all apply this to our lives. Take a look at all the things you do well in your life and if you're feeling under-confident focus on these. Also look at what you can bring from these areas to tackle the problem you're currently undertaking. Taking skills from an area of your life you know you have mastered into an area you feel nervous about will dramatically increase your belief in your abilities and help you do what you want to do.

AVOID NEGATIVE PEOPLE

How are you supposed to like yourself when those around you are putting you down? Paula was in a relationship where her partner would not only put her down but also mentally and physically abuse her. "He'd talk about my weight and my job and tell me I was fat and worthless. I believed him. My sisters both had degrees and good jobs but I had fallen pregnant at sixteen and left school. I felt I'd disgraced the entire family. I didn't think I was good enough to have what they had so I settled for what I could get. My partner didn't help me at all and he'd call me 'fat-cow' and 'lardarse'. If I talked about getting a better job he'd say 'Why? What's the point? You won't get it,' and things like that. When he shouted at me and hit me it was always because of things I'd supposedly done wrong (like running out of milk!). After five years of this I really believed that I deserved everything that happened to me. After all, I'd let my parents down, the most important people to me in the world. Then I met someone else. He thought my figure was beautiful and we'd talk about more than how much he'd drunk that day. I began to realize that I was quite intelligent, that I could hold a conversation and that I might not have any qualifications on paper but that I could hold my own with people that did – and that was what counted. I signed up with a temp agency – I had taken typing at school and after a bit of practice I was up to 60 wpm. They liked me and the people I worked for liked me. Suddenly no one around me was putting me down. They were praising me and this boosted how I felt about myself. One day I decided to take that final step and threw out my partner. Now I'm married to the man I met and I'm still temping but have doubled my hourly rate – I also model for an outsize fashion agency. I realized I didn't have to believe the crap I was being fed any more and that I could believe in myself. But if someone hadn't helped me I'd never have done it myself – too many other people around me didn't believe in me for me to believe in myself."

START LIVING THE CONFIDENT LIFE NOW

The power of confidence is incredible. Even if you don't really believe you have it, acting as if you do can work wonders – just be careful. Lack of confidence can manifest as overacting (talking too loudly or making extreme gestures) or in behaviour not appropriate for a situation. It's therefore far more powerful to look at someone whom you admire for their confidence. Think how they would react to the situation that is making you nervous and try to adopt a version of their behaviour that that fits your personality.

ALWAYS REMEMBER, THE MORE YOU WORK ON CONFIDENCE, THE MORE YOU CAN ACHIEVE

It's not like learning a new language where it's alien to you. You were born confident and liking yourself. Somewhere in your mind, in your body, is your self-confidence and it's waiting to come back.

Guilt

Guilt. It's that sinking feeling in the pit of your stomach that makes you feel sick. It's the constant nagging fear that your actions could have hurt someone else. It's endless nights not sleeping, thinking about something you've done. It's also often a complete waste of time. One-third of the population say they permanently feel guilty. However, about 80 per cent of the time, what we're feeling guilty about is not worth it.

It's true that guilt can be constructive; it's a necessary emotion that allows us to distinguish right from wrong and reflect on the consequence of our actions. Research from Case Western Reserve University in Ohio has revealed that feeling guilty about something they've done can help people change their behaviour for the better. However, guilt comes in two forms, healthy and toxic, and most of the time we experience the latter. Toxic guilt not only wastes huge amounts of time and emotion, it also affects our health. Toxic guilt leads

Who Feels Guilty and About What?

A 1996 study from ARISE looked at people's attitudes in eight countries to 13 everyday pleasures (including alcohol, sex and watching TV) and measured their guilt reaction. Of the countries studied, the Dutch have the most relaxed attitudes to pleasure. The Germans rank bottom in the league for enjoyment and when they do let themselves go they feel more guilty than anyone else in Europe. The British come second for indulging in pleasure – but also score way above average for feeling guilty afterwards. So what hits our guilt buttons? Eating chocolate and other sweet things, doing nothing, not exercising and smoking

to a toxic body with high levels of stress hormones and tension. Professor David Warburton at the Associates for Research into the Science of Enjoyment discovered that guilty feelings suppress the immune system which can lead to illness. Toxic guilt can also take a toll on your life. Those who say they feel guilty experience less pleasure and are generally unhappier than their peers.

Unlike confidence, we weren't born with guilt. It's a learned emotion that psychologists believe starts to develop around the age of three. Why? Do phrases like, "if you leave those toys out again, someone will trip and you'll be sorry," or "if you don't stop wandering off you'll be the death of me," bring to mind anything from your childhood? Our toddler years are when we first develop the ability to tackle our needs personally. The problem is that, because we don't understand the consequences of our actions, the results often lead to lots of negative reinforcement – much of it guilt-related. "The most important thing any parent can do for their child is avoid shaming them," says Tony Schirtzinger. "Phrases like 'what's wrong with you?' or 'why can't you be like so and so who treats his mother right?' lead to negative thinking patterns." Instead of growing up being able to make choices freely, we grow up believing that when we do something that displeases others it leads to a severe negative reaction and that belief lives on in our subconscious. Add to this the fact that we're always taught to put others before ourselves and you have one big recipe for self-recrimination.

"I spend endless time feeling guilty. It leads to sleepless nights, obsessive eating and arguments with my partner," says Maggie. "I can compartmentalize my worry into three main areas. I worry about what I do or don't do to my body (what I eat, drink, smoke and my lack of physical exercise). I feel bad that I haven't got my figure back after having a baby when other women have. I feel guilt about being a working mother – when I'm at work I think about my daughter and when I leave dead on time to go and see her I think about those I've left behind in the office. Finally, I feel guilty because I'm a have, not a have not. I feel bad about people in underprivileged backgrounds. I hate the amount of time I spend on my guilt – and the fact that it materializes with me being angry with my partner and my colleagues. I do try and rationalize it but it doesn't always work. I'm sure if I stopped feeling guilty about my body I'd stop overeating and probably get the figure I wanted. Mind you, I don't want to lose all of my guilt. I think it would make me a hard person. When I feel bad about something I've done to my friends I probably should and if I didn't feel guilty about having more than other people I wouldn't be moved to help them – no one would. That's one area I feel good about feeling bad about. I just wish I could deal with the other areas."

Maggie is trapped by her guilt because she hasn't taken the step towards overcoming it. She has, however, discovered the fundamental principle that will allow her to do this. She can see the difference between healthy guilt and toxic guilt. This is the key to overcoming problems with this debilitating emotion. Differentiating is actually easy – what causes us problems is realizing that we are allowed to do it.

SO HOW DO YOU CHANGE BAD FEELINGS INTO GOOD?

"The real test for most people today is to find something they are not guilty about," says Robert Holden, counsellor and author of *Happiness Now*. "Guilt is so widespread that I would have to say guilt is not so much an emotion as a way of life." Overcoming guilt is not something we expect to do. But it's actually extremely easy. Getting control of your guilt takes just one step. Every time you start to get that niggling in your stomach, ask yourself one question. Ask, "Do I deserve this feeling?" Just sit there and think about what you've done and what the consequences of that action are *really* going to be. Not what you think they're going to be (guilt has a habit of magnifying even the most simple problems into major life-destroyers) but what will actually happen because of what you have done. Now look at this in terms of the level that you're beating yourself up. Should you really allow yourself this much angst over cancelling a drink with a friend tonight? If they're splitting up with their partner and need to talk, then yes you probably should; if all it means is that they have to stay in and watch TV instead, it's not worth it.

If you decide that, yes, you deserve to feel guilty this time, don't wallow in it. Guilt is an emotion not a solution and the only thing that's going to help you here is dealing with it. Think what you can do to make amends for your actions. If you can put any of it into motion do it, if not make a list of the steps it'll take and when you're going to action them – then stop thinking about it until then.

All worry is a waste of time, but guilt-induced worrying is the worst. Either act on something or forget about it.

Then try to prevent it.

Next time that little voice in the back of your head tells you to start feeling bad about something, take a step back and ask yourself the following questions.

WHERE IS THIS GUILT COMING FROM? IS THE VOICE I'M HEARING MINE OR IS IT MY PARENTS'?

You should only feel guilt over an action that goes against your own moral code – just because your father would never have an overdraft doesn't mean you shouldn't have one. "I worked with a businessman who was having terrible trouble sleeping. This was affecting his health and his work," says hypnotherapist and stress counsellor Carole Allen. "I asked him about his parents and discovered that at the root of his problems were feelings of guilt. He was stressed, he knew he was stressed but he had been brought up being told that we didn't show things like that. In 40 years he had never seen his parents have an argument. He really felt that if he showed emotion and lost control he would let his parents down. This resulted in a life where everything was rigidly controlled and the only thing he could have no control over was when he fell asleep. Exploring this and helping him look at what was right for him helped him overcome it." This gentleman's manifestation of guilt may have been slightly unusual, but the reason behind it is exceptionally common. If you do it – stop.

WHAT ARE THE ACTUAL CONSEQUENCES OF WHAT I'VE DONE?

If there isn't any major fallout from your actions, forget it. You can even grade things. Ask how what you've done is going to affect your relationship with the person concerned. Rank the answer on a scale of one to ten. If it's under a six or seven, forget it. If it's above, or you decide that the consequences aren't something you could deal with if it happened to you, determine what you can do to limit the damage.

THINK ABOUT YOURSELF

If you have a guilt-prone personality most things will seem overimportant to you – so judge your actions on how you would feel if someone had done them to you. If the answer is nothing, or that you'd feel fed up for five minutes, why are you obsessing for an hour? "A good exercise for the guilt-prone is to make a list of five or six things you have felt guilt over in the past and ask the people affected by your actions how you made them feel," says counsellor Rita Cottee. "Chances are, something you still feel bad over, they've forgotten about."

WHAT IS THE BIG PICTURE?

If you always tell your kids that you'll go to the park and then work overtime instead, then, yes, you probably should feel guilty. If, however, you're normally there for them but just this once you can't do what you said you'd do, don't obsess over it.

DO THE BENEFITS OF MY ACTIONS OUTWEIGH THE CONSEQUENCES?

Research from ARISE reveals that the one thing most people feel bad about is doing nothing. Yet any health expert will tell you that this is one of the most important things you can do for your mind, your body, your relationship, your career – you name it, time off is good for it. If what you're feeling bad about is going to do you good, forget it. "Clinical studies show that in moderation, pleasure can reduce stress and increase resistance to disease," says Professor David Warbuton from ARISE. So guilt-free indulgence in your favourite treat can relieve stress.

Worry

Worrying is not fear of reality, it's fear of what might happen and, as such, 90 per cent of the things that we worry about are pointless. Okay, so, just like guilt, some level of worry can be good. It can act as a warning system that spurs us into action. You've got an unusual mole on your arm, it worries you, you get it checked, it's removed; you've saved yourself an awful lot of trauma and that's good. Or are you that type of person? Are you the type of person who would have worried about the problem without taking the trip to the doctor? "Worry is good if, as in this case, it alerts you to real danger or if it goads you into some action that has an identifiable results" says counsellor Rita Cottee. "Worry isn't good if it just leads to you wasting time, energy and emotions and offers no solutions."

One of the world's foremost authorities on worrying, Edward Hallowell of the Hallowell Center in Concord, Massachusetts, calls this toxic worry. He believes that up to 15 per cent of us regularly experience this negative emotion – and that 25 per cent of the population may even suffer health problems because of it. Toxic worry leads to increased blood pressure, higher levels of stress hormones and some doctors even link it to cancer. In the short term, worry wastes time; in the mid-term it can lead to conditions like panic attacks (see page 153) and in the long term it could kill you. Do you have the feeling this is something you really need to dejunk?

DO YOU SUFFER FROM TOXIC WORRY?

The answer is yes if what you're experiencing contains one or more of the following:

RICOCHETING. As you think about the sequences of your fears you jump from one negative scenario to another – and each is worse than the last. You can't focus on one outcome and this prevents you from focusing on one solution

For most of us, worry is another one of those developed traits that stunt our emotional growth. However, it's possible that worry could be innate. Researchers from the National Institute of Health in Washington, DC have discovered a genetic defect that acts on serotonin (a calming compound in the brain). This causes two-thirds of the people who carry the gene to be predisposed to feelings of anxiety or other negative emotions. While more research needs to be carried out, doctors believe that one day the discovery of this gene (and their belief that other areas of the brain may also be affected) will help the millions of people around the world who suffer from extreme anxiety disorders such as phobias

PERPETUATING. Toxic worry is like mould, it grows and takes over everything around it. If you start to worry about things you've otherwise been fine about, you're experiencing toxic worry

PROPHESIZING. If your worries all begin "what if", it's toxic worry. You should only ever worry about things that are definitely going to happen – and soon

NEGATIVITY. Good worry feels positive – it spurs you into action and makes you think of solutions. Toxic worry just makes you feel bad

FIXATING. If what you are worrying about is all you can think about, yet it's not in proportion to the effect it will have on your life – or if people comment on how much you worry generally, you have a problem with toxic worry.

The problem with worrying about everything is that what goes through our heads creates the world that we live in. If you start to believe that everything is going to get bad, it may well do that. Not least because you're so concerned about what could happen you don't actively take any steps to prevent it – which is where dejunking comes in. You can lower your levels of worry and get things to a state where you can work things out, not just obsess about them.

WORRY-FREE WAYS TO BEAT ANXIETY

1 GET THE FACTS. Worrying about anything when you do not have all the facts is always going to be a waste of time. Get all the info, then think it through.

2 ASK IF YOUR WORRY IS ONE OF THE THREE U'S. Is it Unimportant, Unlikely or Unresolvable? If so, it shouldn't be worried about. You should also ask yourself:

- Is what I'm worrying about going to matter in six months' time?
- Is what I'm worrying about definitely or extremely likely to happen?
- Can I actually do anything about it anyway?

If the answer to any of these is no, the problem isn't worth worrying about.

3 ACT ON THE WORRY. Anything that is actually worth worrying about can be dealt with, and putting this in motion is one of the most powerful dejunk tools. Look at how you can tackle your worry. Break this down into easy steps – then take that first step. Say you're concerned about the amount you owe on your credit card; you need a plan that can realistically help you pay it off. Step one is working this out. Step two is making an appointment with your bank manager. Most of us worry about things at night when we can't do anything about them, but don't forget answerphones. Calling the bank voicemail and leaving a message to say you'd like to make an appointment and can someone call you tomorrow will alleviate so much pressure that you might get some sleep. If you can do something, do it.

One in every twenty people experience regular panic attacks. The condition is characterized by episodes of speeding heart rate, sweating, tingling fingers and faster breathing. Attacks often happen when people are under stress or high levels of anxiety but the psychological trigger for those prone to panic attacks can be minute. One famous study asked people to read out words in pairs – and for people prone to panic attacks even just reading pairs like 'breathless and choking' was enough to trigger an attack. Doctors don't really know what causes them – one recent study even found a link with the weather – but it's believed to be an overreaction to stimuli around the person. Often the first attack comes without warning and the sufferer believes they are going to faint or are having a heart attack. This fear – of either making a fool of themselves or, in the extreme, dying – means next time they experience a similar sensation they panic – which can bring on another attack. However, you can beat them

KNOW THE FACTS. The thing most people fear is what the attack will lead to but panic can't make you faint and it won't kill you. Once people realize that, a lot of fear can be prevented

DON'T TAKE DEEP BREATHS. The tingling is caused by an excess of oxygen in the system and you actually need to lower the oxygen in your body. Breathing slowly in and out of a paper bag can help as this increases your intake of carbon dioxide

DON'T TRY AND CONTROL THE ATTACK BUT LIVE THROUGH IT CONSCIOUSLY. One of the most important parts of panic-attack treatment is asking people to work through an attack to the end. This makes you realize that you can come through it okay. The next time it's done with more attention to thoughts and feelings. Eventually people understand what's happening. They stay calm through the attack and the fear that magnifies the reaction leaves them – reducing both the severity and frequency of attacks

4 THEN DO SOMETHING ELSE. Not every worry you've ever had in your life resolves itself but can you remember what you worried about as a child? Your mind only has so much room for things. If you can do something else you'll stop thinking about your worry. One of the best things you can do is go somewhere different. Take a walk or a run, for example. "If you change your physical state you change your mental one," says Edward Hallowell.

5 TALK ABOUT IT. Women are far more likely to do this than men – but it's true that a problem shared is a problem halved. First it allows perspective but it also increases the chance of finding a solution. And don't worry, you won't upset your friends – worry is not catching.

Negative Thinking

"What you believe will be how you live," says Robert Holden. "You are entirely faithful to your conscious and unconscious beliefs. What you believe is also what you perceive. If you think the world is a bad place, you will see it only as such. Change what you believe and you change what you see and you change the pattern of your life." The trouble is, we are conditioned to see and think about the negative things in our lives. Just look at our speech patterns. We say we're "not so bad" or "we're getting by". We feel "no news is good news". We even express happiness in negative terms "having a terribly good time". Negativity is our natural way of thinking. Take something as simple as having a headache, no one ever says, "Well the rest of me feels fine but my head hurts;" Instead we concentrate on the thing that's giving us pain and this attitude follows us through every area of our lives. We could experience 100 good things in a day and forget every one of them, but we'd remember the one bad thing that happened. I once interviewed a leading breast-cancer surgeon for a magazine piece. The man was brilliant, he had saved thousands of women's lives over the decades of his career, but he admitted the ones he couldn't help haunted him and that he had had trouble with that. "In the end I began to realize that I had to forget about them, which was dreadful as this was someone's life we were talking about here," he told me. "Instead, I had to learn to see each day as a new challenge and look for the good in it. I began to concentrate on the strides we were making in medical research, the fact that the death rate was falling and that I was playing some small part in that. I learnt I had to concentrate on the positive, otherwise I would never be able to transmit that to my patients."

This attitude is something the rest of us should take on. We might not be dealing with life and death, but we do have to learn to get out from under the cloud of negativity and accentuate the positive things in our life. Take a look at the statements below. Each one identifies a common pattern of negative thinking. Look at the words outside the brackets and see if you can see these patterns in your speech. You may fall into one area – you may span more than one. Some may affect different areas of your life. But if you are prone to any of them, they are holding you back and you need to dejunk your thinking.

TYPE 1

•"Well, I (messed up that presentation), I might as well (resign now)."

•"I'm constantly (arguing with my partner about the wedding arrangements). If we can't even get that right, I (don't know how he thinks we're going to make a marriage work)."

This is categorical thinking. If you're prone to this, chances are you put everything in your life into pigeonholes. If one thing in your life goes wrong, you believe that everything else in that area of your life is also bad. It leads to negative feelings about life in general and often precipitates negative events. Categorical thinkers tend to be rigid in their beliefs and convinced there's only one right solution – again this can hold you back. "The more ways you can think of to deal with a problem, the more likely you are to solve it – and the more successful the results are likely to be," says counsellor Rita Cottee.

TYPE 2

•"I'm not thinking about how (I'm going to spend the £100 I won on the lottery) until I get it. There might be a mistake (on the ticket) and it might never happen."

•"Oh great, I've got to (meet my new boss on Monday). I never (work well on a Monday)."

Negativity v depression?

Sometimes what we believe to be negative thinking patterns are actually symptoms of depression, which is much harder to overcome. Many people believe depression is just a case of the blues. It's not. Depression is often described as a black cloud or a black hole and sufferers really believe that nothing they or anyone around them does can lift them out of it. Depressed people feel hopeless and will express their options and choices in life as hopeless – they honestly believe they don't have any. Eventually many stop thinking or talking about their worries and act as if they don't care about themselves or those around them. Depression can also lead to changes in the body chemistry which trigger problems like loss of appetite, lethargy and increased need to sleep. There are many types of depression and many cures, both medicinal and psychological. The first step to beating it is to seek help. See your GP or contact one of the organizations listed in the resources section of this book

- "He's (an Aries), I'm (a Sagittarius). It's doomed from the start."

You suffer from superstitious thinking. This is one area where it's very easy for our mind to influence us. A good example of this is a sportsman who will wear a particular item or go through a certain ritual before an event to ensure good luck. If that ritual is disturbed or their talisman is lost they don't believe they can win – and invariably they don't. The reason has nothing to do with luck. Its because their mind won't let them. Many of us can work in the same way. Say we believe we always function more slowly on a Monday – then we will. Superstitious thinking can also be blamed for holding us back. " 'I'll do that if' is a common phrase in the superstitious vocabulary," says Rita Cottee. "It can stop us taking risks and can prevent us from taking advantage of everything life has to offer us."

TYPE 3

- "I can't get this (drawer to stop sticking). I don't know why I bother anyway. The whole (house) is falling apart. It's never going to work."

- "I can't stop arguing with Joe about (taking the rubbish out). If we can't deal with anything that simple it's clearly not working. We might as well quit now."

You suffer from fogging: With foggers, when one thing in their life goes wrong it's almost as if a fog descends over their thinking and clouds it. They don't distinguish between problems, so something simple triggers an overreaction and affects everything else. Soon the fogger begins to lose touch with what actually caused the problem in the first place. If a fogger has a row with a partner over who is going to do the washing up, the fogger will see this as a sign that that the partner doesn't value the same things. If you can't even agree about your various housework roles, how the hell are you going to come to terms with something like having children? Before you know it, you've decided that the two of you are destined for the divorce court. It's almost as if, as you stumble around in the fog, you bump into every other problem you've ever had in that part of your life. "Foggers are often scared of rejection and may have low self-esteem," says Rita Cottee. "It's almost like a pre-emptive strike. 'Let me do the hurting or make the final decision, that way I'm in control.'" Foggers are their own worst enemies. By always assuming the worst, they can actually rob themselves of many positive opportunities and experiences.

TYPE 4

- "I can't go out until (I've cleaned this room up) but by then it'll be too late to go."

- "I've managed to (lose a stone for my holiday) but I was supposed (to lose two) so that was a waste of time."

You're a perfectionist. "I must", "I should" and "I have to" are all common phrases in the perfectionist thinker's vocabulary. Perfectionist thinking can work against you because you can never be pleased. You set yourself high goals which are often unrealistic and so you will never measure up to what you're trying to do. Constantly dotting I's and crossing T's wastes time and energy. You're more likely to fixate on the details and never see the whole picture.

TYPE 5

- "What's the point in my (approaching that woman over there). I never manage to (attract women I like the look of). And even if I did (she'd probably dump me after the first date)."

- "I'm not going to (apply for that new job). Everyone knows that (they give jobs to people they know). You only get things in life if you know someone or you're lucky – and I'm not."

You're a pessimist. Pessimists always look on the dark side of life. If something bad happens it is always their fault – if they got knocked over it's because they didn't look, not because the car pulled out of a blind space at 40 miles an hour. On the other end of the scale, pessimists never take credit for the good things they have done – if they cook a great meal, for example, it'll be the recipe or the poor quality of their dinner guests' tastebuds that led to its success rather than their culinary expertise. Being a pessimist is one of the most destructive ways of thinking there is. "There's no pay-off for being a pessimist," says Robert Holden. "I describe them as people who die before they die. By breaking out of the trap your life can really be what you want it to be."

SO HOW DO YOU GET OUT OF THE TRAP?

Although each negative thinking pattern has different characteristics, they almost all respond to the same techniques. The good news is that by applying positive thinking and positive steps you can change how you think. Some doctors believe change can occur in just a few weeks.

1 RECOGNIZING YOUR THINKING PATTERN IS THE FIRST STEP TOWARDS GETTING OUT OF IT

Now you're primed to look for those phrases you will be more aware of what you are doing. When you find yourself thinking categorically, or pessimistically, stop and hold that thought. Think – what is the result of thinking that way? Is that the consequence that I actually want to come out of that situation? If the answer is no, go against your initial thought. Turn it on its head or on its side but don't fall into the trap. The more you work against it, the less engrained the habit will be.

2 LOOK AT WHY YOU ARE DOING IT

"It's the answer to almost every psychological problem," says Rita Cottee. "The reasons for doing specific things are extremely powerful. Often negative thinking patterns can be avoidance techniques. Ways to not face up to what's really wrong or ways to protect yourself against failure or rejection. Look at what's really behind your thinking patterns and tackle that."

3 THINK WORST-CASE SCENARIO

"This is often the best way to overcome fear," says Rita Cottee. "Look at what the worst possible thing that could happen to you in that situation is – could you live with it? Often, the fear of the unknown is far worse than what would happen if we faced up to things." Then think of the best possible scenario. Creating positive fantasies in our mind not only helps us to think of solutions that may solve our problems and helps us achieve our dreams, it also helps us get used to thinking of ourselves in positive terms. If the little voice says, "Yes, but that'll never happen," ignore it. No, you might never marry a millionaire or win the lottery but that doesn't mean that those positive money vibes might not be transmitted into other areas of your life.

4 TAKE THE RISK

Try and beat negative thinking patterns by taking the steps you are trying to avoid. You have already looked at what the worst is that could happen. You know how you would deal with that, so why not go for it? "If you're going to have a simpler life you have to give up being a victim and take some chances," says Robert Holden.

Suppressed Emotions

"The average person gets angry about twenty times a day but if you ask them many swear they never get angry at all," says Tony Schirtzinger. "Anger is one of the emotions we are most likely to suppress yet doing so does us no favours whatsoever." In fact, it could kill us. Research recently discovered that people who suppress anger and other emotions were far more likely to develop thickening of the carotid arteries than those who let things out. This thickening can increase the risk of thrombosis and heart disease – and all because you didn't shout when you needed to.

According to Tony Schirtzinger, the top five most suppressed emotions are anger, joy, sadness, fear and excitement. However, he explains that all of our feelings can be suppressed. "Some people have been trained to show positive emotions and hide negative ones, others reveal everything, others suppress everything." How you react is determined by a complex interplay of factors, including the way your family dealt with emotions, and past experience of expressing emotions (children whose parents chastized them for crying or being too exuberant are very prone to suppression). Our culture trains us not to express emotions, as do some religions. Finally, even your state of mind and health can determine how you are going to react to a situation and whether you'll let rip or

Five Minute Psych Tip: Mindful Decision Making

If you're worried about something, acting on it is the best thing you can do. However, when your mind's under pressure it can be hard to make that decision. Mindful decision making can help by structuring your thoughts

• Rule 1: don't think of the consequences of a decision as right or wrong. If you think that you could fail at what you do you'll be less likely to take that risk. See the decision you make and carry out as your success – the outcome of that isn't always something you can control. Realizing there's no right or wrong answer is very important if you're going to focus

• Rule 2: brainstorm. Look at what you are worrying about and think of all the ways you could deal with it. From the obvious to the bizarre. The more options you can come up with the more in control you'll feel. Now look at which is right for you. Look at all the things you want to achieve from your decision and work out which fulfils the most

not. Generally, the more stressed or unhappy you are, and the worse your health, the more likely you are to express emotions – sadly, you'll refer to it as losing control.

Calling this natural expression "loss of control" reflects our attitude to emotions. In the UK particularly, we are told that expressing feelings is rude or weak. However, no one has told our bodies this. When your body is exposed to an emotion, a complex interplay of hormones occurs which gets the body ready to express that emotion – if you then hold it back you don't release those hormones and your body exists in a heightened emotional state which can only lead to negative consequences. And these consequences are many – those who don't express emotions are less likely to have fulfilling relationships as their intimacy response is dampened. You could find it harder to get on at work as people won't tell you the truth about your performance. We tend to give criticism to people who criticize us – people who hide emotions are usually seen as too nice to handle it. You could also find problems rising up the career ladder because of your inability to tell others how you feel about their performance. Without expressing our emotions we are only half people. "A life without awareness of feelings is dull and lifeless at best," says Tony Schirtzinger. "We have to realize the importance of showing what we feel. Suppressed emotions never go away. They just take a toll on us emotionally or physically."

If we've grown up being told that expressing emotions is wrong, how do we then switch ourselves into confessional mode?

1 FACE UP TO THE FACT THAT YOU HAVE A NEGATIVE SIDE

"We all have one," says counsellor and author Gael Lindenfield. "And if we don't recognize this it only comes out in our subconscious. Accepting and acknowledging that we do get angry or sometimes don't like people are essential to emotional and physical health. One way Gael says you can help come to terms with this side of your personality is to make a list of negative questions. Things like: what's the worst thing you've ever done? What would people say is your worst trait? What would *you* say is your worst trait? If you wrote graffiti on a wall what would they say? By looking at your responses to these, you can start to face up to the fact that you're not perfect – but that it doesn't make you a bad person. "It can also help you work out where the negative feelings are coming from – which is the first step in learning to overcome them," she explains.

2 LEARN TO IDENTIFY YOUR FEELINGS

Often we ascribe the wrong emotions to feelings, which doesn't help us express things. We feel guilt instead of anger over suffering in the third world; we worry over a mistake we've made instead of feeling remorse. To express feelings correctly you have to determine you're reacting in the correct way. Tony Schirtzinger believes that different emotions are physically experienced in different places on our body – for example, the lump in your throat that accompanies sadness, the sinking feeling that accompanies worry. Learning where each feeling is held and how it feels helps you come to terms with your emotions.

3 LOOK AT THE SOURCE

Until you understand why you find it hard to reveal how you really feel, you are never going to get past your internal belief that doing so is wrong.

4 GIVE IT A TRY

"If you have a dozen people in the same situation, chances are you will all be feeling the same thing," says Rita Cottee. "There's an empathy there. It's not like you're going to be seen as feeling something completely different from the others. You just have to be strong enough to admit to the person nearest (or closest) to you how you feel. Often they will then respond."

5 EVEN IF YOU'RE ALONE

If you don't think you can face other people with your emotions, work on them alone. Hitting a pillow, even shouting at the person you're angry with in the mirror to yourself at least gets the feeling out in the open.

How to be Happy

Now you've got this far, technically you should be happy! According to happiness researcher Dr Michael Argyle at Oxford University, the major

How to Cry

One of the most important ways to release pent-up emotion is to cry, but many of us – especially men – find it extremely hard to do. Realistically, crying is good for you, it relaxes muscles, lowers blood pressure and acts almost as a natural tranquilizer, but there are good ways to cry and bad ways. Crying alone is seen as negative, as it doesn't allow you to reveal what you are upset about, it allows you to dwell on your fears and negative emotions and makes it unlikely you will work things through. It's more healthy to cry with someone who can talk you through your feelings. If you find this hard and need to sob in solitude, make sure you talk to someone shortly afterwards about what was making you feel bad. This helps to release tension. Crying is also negative if it's used to replace the correct emotion you should feel in a situation. Crying is normally an expression of sadness or grief. If you are angry or stressed about something you should be dealing with these emotions; crying will not get to the root of the problem

sources of happiness are fulfilling relationships, a sense of achievement at work and enjoyable leisure time. Other researchers add mental traits like high self-esteem, a sense of personal control and an optimistic outlook to the mix. Therefore, you can see that if you've worked through this book and everything's gone the way I hope it will, you should be feeling pretty good internally and externally by now. "The biggest key to unlocking happiness is to live for the moment," says Robert Holden. "You can't keep thinking, 'I'll be happy tomorrow,' because tomorrow may never come. Think what you can do to be happy now and you'll always be happy." Experts say that even creating feelings of instant pleasure are enough to generate the release of "happy hormones" in the brain and set the physiological processes of feeling good in motion. So what's the key to instant happiness?

ANIMALS

Unconditional love, someone to talk to and the stress-relieving effects of animal interaction explain why animals scored so highly when Hull University asked what made people happy.

SMILING AND LAUGHING

A study by California Medical School showed that even fake smiling and laughing release endorphins (the happy hormones) into the brain. By faking a smile or a laugh you stimulate the physiological reactions that lead to happiness in the body – and immediately improve your mood.

EXERCISE

A study by *Self* magazine found that 93 per cent of people who exercise say they are happy when they're doing it. The reason is that exercise releases endorphins. "The results of twenty minutes of exercise last for up to two hours afterwards," says trainer Luke Wilkins.

MUSIC AND DANCING

Music has huge effects on emotions and mood and, combined with the physical activity of dancing, it's no wonder Michael Argyle believes it's a powerful instant "happifier".

IF ALL ELSE FAILS – JUST MOVE TO ICELAND

Every year, researchers compile a list of the happiest countries in the world – and Iceland wins every year!

Just one final thing. While the above advice may have come from experts, no book can completely "cure" someone with really deep-set negative beliefs. Such a person needs personal attention. A list of organizations providing referrals to therapists and counsellors can be found in the resources section. Seeking help doesn't mean you're weak, nor does it mean you have a "mental illness" or are "going mad". Look at it this way, if two people were bleeding badly, who would you think was sane – the one who sought help, or the one who ignored their injuries because they were embarrassed? The only difference between seeking help for a physical illness and mental distress is that you hurt in a different part of your body.

Summary

The mind is like a magnet. What we believe determines how our life will be. By changing negative thinking patterns you can dramatically alter the way you think about your life and therefore the path it will take

The most common traits that hold back your mind are: low self-confidence, guilt, worry, suppressed emotions and negative thinking

Most of us are actually happy. We just don't realize it yet

Action Plan

Use the ABC model to identify your patterns of thinking. Are you happy with this?

If not, work through each of the areas in which you feel you need to dejunk your mind. Always remember those negative thought-patterns took a long time to develop but you can change them.

Concentrate on being happy today

Chapter 9
Dejunk Your Love Life

ALL RELATIONSHIPS *are extremely powerful. Whether it be our friends, our families or our partners, the events and emotions transmitted between us can positively or negatively affect every element of our lives. How many times have you argued with your partner before leaving the house in the morning and found your entire working day thrown out of synch until you've managed to contact them and patch things up? How often do you find that when you are in touch with your family, old feuds or even engrained patterns of behaviour come to the fore, affecting the outcome of a situation almost before the first step has taken place? Why is it that talking to a close friend can always make you feel better when you're down – even though they don't actually solve any problems?*

Why Do We Need to Dejunk Our Love Lives?

The truth is relationships can affect our lives positively and negatively, but the more social contact you have the better your life is likely to be. People with lots of friends are happier than those without, and this helps us in our jobs and our day-to-day interactions. You're more likely to feel positive mentally – suicide rates among unmarried men and women are dramatically higher than among those with partners, for example; and you're definitely going to be healthier physically. People who have lots of social support and friendships are likely to be healthier and live longer than those who describe themselves as lonely or isolated. The benefits include everything from catching fewer colds (as proven by Swedish research) to being up to five times less likely to suffer serious ailments such as heart disease. However, this doesn't mean you should just head off and make new friends left right and centre. The key to life-benefiting relationships is positivity.

So What Does This Mean for You?

Does it mean that if you're in an unhappy marriage you're going to die? Or that because you didn't get on with your parents as a child you're doomed to heart problems. Not necessarily. What matters is how those relationships affect you from now on. According to leading heart-disease researcher Dean Ornish, it's not what happened to us in the past that matters, but the ongoing pattern of our relationships in the future. Dejunking your relationships is about improving that ongoing pattern. It's about getting rid of the relationships that really don't work in your life and teaching you how to get the most out of those that do. The amount of time and energy that even a healthy relationship wastes on negativity is phenomenal. Even otherwise happy families or spouses can find themselves having the same arguments over and over again, but by learning to dejunk your relationships you can take control.

So Where Do You Start?

Before you can start to dejunk your relationships you need to look objectively at what state they are in at present – something I call a relationship audit. This is not an easy exercise. One of the biggest reasons that so many people limp along in negative relationships is that they are terrified about what will happen if they start to explore what's going on. Opening up relationships for scrutiny can bring out a lot of problems you'd rather not face. It can be hard to tell a friend of ten years that you now have nothing in common and that you don't want to be part of their life any more. The guilt can be phenomenal. If you tell your partner to shape up, have you got the self-confidence to go it alone if they say no? This is why, before you actively start tackling relationships, you should dejunk your mind. Working on the two areas in conjunction with each other is going to create far better results than dejunking your relationships alone.

THE RELATIONSHIP AUDIT

STEP 1: DO A HEAD COUNT. Most of us think relationships mean family, partners or just close friends, but when relationship researchers do a relationship audit they cast the net a lot wider than that. They count anyone with whom you have some kind of social contact. This means partners, family, children, friends – but it could also be the client with whom you always chat a little while longer than necessary; a neighbour who always goes out of their way to be nice to you, or other members at a church or a club you go to. For a month or so, note down how many people you make some kind of friendly social contact with – and all those you would normally speak to pretty regularly but haven't managed to this month (like that friend you're avoiding).

STEP 2: NOW LOOK AT THEIR ROLE IN YOUR LIFE. Everyone we encounter in our day has a role. With a partner, for example, it's to support and nurture us, to serve our emotional and physical needs. With someone like a neighbour, it's to pass time and pleasantries with and perhaps rely on for simple tasks like watering plants while you're away. Look at the role you think every person on that list should play in your life – the role that, in an ideal world, you'd like them to have. This may well be different from the one they do have. If you'd prefer that client to be more of a friend, someone you could meet for drinks on a social level, write that down. If your sister-in-law is very needy and calls once a week, when you'd be happier with once a month (or frankly not at all), write that down. If you want your partner to be more physical towards you, write it down. Don't be governed by what you think is right, by emotions like guilt or by any assumptions about that person's personality and willingness to change, just write down what you would like that person's role in your life to be.

STEP 3: DO THEY FULFIL IT? Take each person in turn and ask yourself that question. Some of these will be easy – people to whom you like chatting but don't want to get to know any further work in their relationship role and so you can cross them off the list. A happy marriage with no problems doesn't need any dejunking. But if you find there are contradictions between the roles you'd like people to have and those they perform, these are the areas you need to work on. Over the next two chapters we'll deal with some of the most common ways to do this.

Dejunk Your Partnerships

We've already shown that having a happy relationship with your spouse or partner is good for you – so why is it out of reach for so many of us? One in four marriages ends in divorce, and marriage rates are decreasing. A quarter of married people say they would have an affair if they thought they could get away with it. But how many of these unhappy couples are in unsalvageable relationships or relationships that just need dejunking? By dejunking your relationship you learn to stop spending time dwelling on what's wrong in your relationship and to spend time fixing it instead. It doesn't have to be a major "I'm leaving you" problem. Even the happiest relationships could do with a little bit of streamlining. In a world where we have little enough time with our partner as it is, why do we spend so much of it having the same fight or wondering just why our partner only listens to half of what we say? Dejunking teaches us to deal with the negative and accentuate the positive in a relationship. If something can't be fixed in a relationship you either have to forget about that problem or forget about the relationship.

SO HOW DO YOU KNOW WHAT YOU NEED?

Every relationship goes through bad phases. They are not a problem. The problem is that we focus on them. As in every area of our life, we're trained to look at the negative parts of relationships and forget the positive. You're far more likely to remember the points in a day where your partner doesn't speak to you for an hour than the other fourteen hours when they did. A bad phase does not mean the relationship is over. One bad trait does not mean the relationship is over. Lots of people bail out on relationships because they don't realize just how simple the problem is to solve. Of the top six reasons marriages end, I'd estimate 90 per cent of cases could be prevented by talking about what's going on when it starts. A relationship should only be ended if whatever problems you are having have irreversibly affected its core values – or, because that relationship just can't make you happy again no matter what you do to it. How do you know this? The following questions will help you find out.

HOW DOES THE PROBLEM MANIFEST ITSELF?

If you're merely feeling vague dissatisfaction with the relationship or if you are deciding that your partner is feeling some kind of dissatisfaction, then hold back before you do anything about it. Feelings can be extremely deceptive and one of the most dangerous things you can do in any relationship is second-guess your partner. In fact, relationships where couples do this are among the most likely to fail. If you think there is something wrong with your partner, ask them – don't beat yourself up over something that could be linked to them getting a parking ticket. Also, if you can't pinpoint where your problem with the relationship lies, it may not be the relationship that's causing the problem. If something's wrong between you and your partner you'll know it, even faintly. If you can't quite work it out, carry on through the questions and you'll probably find the answer. If, however, the problem is manifesting itself in frequent arguments or negative behaviour, the reasons why need to be addressed and analyzed. These are not signs of a happy

NOT THINKING ALIKE. A study at Elizabethan College in Pennsylvania asked couples to select from a list of issues those which they found more important and interesting. The romantic couples picked the same issues but when it came to the discussion they had different opinions on them. It's may be that knowing that you can think differently helps you cope better when you disagree on relationship areas

THE STABILITY OF YOUR UPBRINGING. Work published in the *Journal of Marriage and the Family* found that your family background could affect your marriage. The more of the following you experienced, the more likely your own marriage will work: your parents' marriage was happy; you get on with your siblings; you had little conflict with your parents

HOW OFTEN YOU FIDGET WHEN YOU TALK. The less you do this, the better. Research by Dr John Gottman found that the faster a couple's hearts beat, the more they sweat, or the more they fidget, the more likely it is that their relationship would fail

BEING INDEPENDENT. More US research found that spouses who felt greater independence in their marriage were happier than those who were joined at the hip

relationship, but often they can be worked out before serious damage is done. If the problem is manifesting itself in physical or mental abuse, there's no question. It's not a bad phase, it's a bad relationship. You need to seek expert help or get out.

HOW LONG HAS THE PROBLEM BEEN GOING ON?

If it has only been a couple of weeks, then it's a bad patch. Dealing with it now could stop the problem setting off a chain reaction that'll then turn things into a bad relationship. When looking at how long something's been going on, you should look at where you were in the relationship when it started. Experts have pinpointed a number of danger times when you're more likely to find faults in your partner. Four months is one big danger date as this is often when the first glow of a relationship wears off. Two years is another hotspot. Known as "commit or quit time", this is when you could find yourself trying to get out of a relationship where you're unsure of your status. Make sure you know how you feel before you go any further. If the problems have been going on since you got together, it could be a bad relationship. Think how much time and effort you have put in trying to resolve the problem – is the relationship really worth that effort? Do the other elements give you enough pleasure to keep going? If the answer is no, it's a bad relationship and you need to get out.

WHAT ELSE IS GOING ON IN YOUR LIFE?

"Relationships are an area of our life on which we find it easy to project our feelings of unhappiness in other areas," says relationship psychologist Susan Quilliam. "We expect a partner to tolerate negativity more than we would someone like a boss or a friend that is annoying us. We can therefore take things out on a relationship – or even transfer negative feelings. If you're feeling down in a relationship, make sure that really is why you're depressed." Also check out what's going on in the love life of your friends. If friends are particularly happy or unhappy, it makes us react more critically to our own situations.

WHO WOULD HAVE TO CHANGE TO SOLVE THIS PROBLEM?

If the answer is you, then dejunking is definitely possible. If the answer is your partner you have a harder battle. "You can't change another person," says marriage guidance counsellor Lucy Selleck. "They have to want to do it themselves." However, often changing your own behaviour can be enough to dejunk some relationships. How different would you feel about things if instead of noticing ways that say to you that your partner doesn't love you, you start looking for ways they show they do.

AND HOW WOULD THEY HAVE TO CHANGE?

"If to dejunk the relationship means asking someone to change their behaviour, it's possible," says Lucy Selleck. "Even small changes can make enormous differences in a relationship." If someone loves you enough they should be willing to change their behaviour for you. However, if dejunking involves you or your partner changing either your attitudes or personality, it's not going to work in the long run. You'll be living your life as something you are not and that never works.

WHAT DO YOUR FRIENDS THINK OF THE RELATIONSHIP?

Often other people can see the good in situations that we think are hopeless. "I thought Greg and I had nothing in common because whenever we went out, he'd go to one side of the room and I'd go to the other. We would not meet up until hometime," says Katie. "This didn't seem normal to me and I thought he couldn't actually care that much for me if he'd rather be with his friends than me. Then one of my friends pointed out how often we looked at each other while we were apart and how we always touched as we walked past. I did these things unconsciously and hadn't even registered them. We might not have been together but we were completely connected – and it took someone outside the relationship to see that." Just be careful whom you ask – you have to choose a friend who supports you through good and bad. "Some people enjoy other people's misery," says life coach Eileen Mulligan. "You don't want to take that person's advice."

DO YOU GENERALLY HAVE MORE GOOD TIMES THAN BAD TIMES?

All relationships are positive and negative – so long as these generally occur equally, there may not be insurmountable problems.

HAVE THE PROBLEMS OCCURRED BECAUSE ONE OR OTHER OF YOU HAS CHANGED?

Change is one of the biggest problems in any kind of relationship – be it sexual or platonic. We choose people to spend time with because they reflect our likes and our needs and if one person in a relationship changes, the other one can find it very hard to handle. When Jenny lost 7 stone in weight, her husband changed from being loving and supportive to abusive and jealous. "He would accuse of me of trying to attract men and eventually of having an affair with a man at work. Yes, I was dressing differently and I was more confident and going out more, but that was because for the first time in eight years I was happy with myself. He'd always had the upper hand in the relationship because I felt so bad, but now that had changed and he couldn't handle it. I tried to make things work, but I realized the only way he'd be happy again was if I gained weight and I couldn't do that. I realized that what I had thought was a happy marriage only felt happy because I was so miserable about the rest of my life. After a year of trying to work things out I made the decision to leave. It was horrible and bitter, but I'm glad I did it." The most common conflict-causing changes are those in attitudes (we tend to become more conservative as we get older); physical changes; and changes in status and circumstances. Women are also more likely to change than men as the responsibilities of child-rearing and added burdens of work pressures mean we feel we have to grow up sooner than our partners.

WHAT DOES YOUR PARTNER THINK?

If you don't know their opinion of the problem you are never going to solve it. If you can't ask them about the problem, the relationship has a fundamental flaw. Sometimes it can be helpful to write things down to get started. One exercise which therapists recommend is to compile a list of reasons for staying in the relationship and a list of things which would make you leave it. Award stars to each of these to determine how much of a problem you think something is. Ask your partner to do the same – then you can see where you agree there's a problem (usually the easiest to work out) and where only one of you thinks there is trouble. These are more likely to be the ones that lead to a break-up. If one partner doesn't understand how the other is feeling, things are more likely to escalate. Once you know how both of you feel, you can work on solving the problem.

WHY ARE YOU STILL THERE?

You're having a problem, you're not happy with what's going on – ask yourself why you're still there and listen to the first answer that flashes into your head. If this sounds anything like "because I'm scared to leave","because he/she wouldn't cope without me" or "because I couldn't afford the mortgage if I kicked them out", you have a problem. If the answer is "because I love them", there's something here that can be worked out.

The Top Five Relationship Problems and How to Solve Them

Chances are that if you have a problem you can work at, it falls into one of the categories below. These have been identified by Relate as some of the areas most likely to cause problems in a relationship.

- **Communication difficulties**
- **Sexual problems**
- **Affairs**
- **Disagreements over children**
- **Outside influences (such as friends or family)**

Over the next few pages you'll find tactics to help deal with each of these.

1 COMMUNICATION DIFFICULTIES

Not knowing what the other person wants – or knowing what they want but not knowing how to provide it – is the number one problem with relationships. Sometimes it's our own fault. We don't like to rock the boat in any of our relationships. If we don't talk about what's wrong, we won't have to deal with its consequences. Many couples won't talk about things they know are wrong with their relationship for fear of what the outcome might be. However, aside from our fears, there is also the problem that sometimes even the closest couples just don't understand each other. The big problem is that we are always taught "do as you would be done by". Our parents tell us to treat people as we would like to be treated; so when there's a problem we tend to try and solve it in the way we would like someone to help us. If you're an open person you'll try and get the other person to talk about how they are feeling (when they might want to wallow in their own misery). If you're a more introverted type you may want to leave your partner alone when they are angry or upset about something because you hate to be disturbed. If they are the open type this is a big mistake and only causes further hurt. So how can you resolve the issues?

UNDERSTAND WHY YOU BOTH COMMUNICATE THE WAY YOU DO

"Like many things in our life, our communication skills can be affected by our upbringing," says Susan Quilliam. "A child in a family of parents who argued a lot would have closed their ears when things got frightening. When they become an adult, they do the same. It can be very hard to break out of this kind of pattern so adapting your communication skills will help reduce conflict." Think about why you shout, why you stay silent, why you find it hard to express your feelings. Look at what is hardest to break and talk to your partner about why you can't do it.

ACTUALLY LISTEN TO YOUR PARTNER

I often accuse my boyfriend of being like the dog in *The Simpsons*. In one episode, Santa's Little Helper is listening to people and all he can understand are phrases like biscuit, blah, blah, blah, walk, blah, blah, blah and vet. In my boyfriend's case all he hears is dinner, blah, blah, blah, beer, blah, blah, holiday, blah, blah, but as for the bits in between, I could be offering to poison him with his dinner, buy beer to celebrate and go on holiday with the life insurance. He hasn't got a clue. Most of the time I ignore it but when I want to talk about something important my tone changes and he listens. Obviously no one can give their partner undivided time, we'd get suffocated, but learn to pick up on the clues that say it's serious.

NEVER SECOND-GUESS YOUR PARTNER

Don't assume you know what they're thinking, or what they are going to say or do next. Often this leads to misunderstandings as you think you've heard something, or you think, "That's what they really meant to say, because that's what they always say".

GO BACK TO THE BEGINNING OF YOUR RELATIONSHIP AND LOOK HOW YOU COMMUNICATED THEN

"Finding out how people think and feel, and how they got to where they were when you met them is crucial to a developing relationship, but as we grow comfortable with each other we don't ask this kind of question any more," says Susan Quilliam. "We should. If you don't ask your partner how they feel, you won't know. It may feel strange at first, but the more you practise the 'interview' technique the easier it will become – and the more your relationship can grow."

HOW TO HAVE A FAIR FIGHT

Arguing is a part of most relationships – even the strongest ones. In fact, research has revealed that couples who never argue are more likely to break up than those who row once or twice a week. However, you have to argue properly otherwise you can go round and round in circles with an argument and end up causing more problems than you solve. When you have an argument, something good should come out of it – you should use it to solve a problem, otherwise you'll just row about it again. Consider the following:

SHOULD YOU BE ARGUING ABOUT THIS AT ALL? How important is the issue in the scheme of your relationship? Is it worth getting angry over? If it's a one-off, then no. If you're sure it's a symptom of something larger, then it's worth at least trying to talk about it. Any argument which is started just because you're in the mood, or want to prove you're right, is going nowhere. As a general rule, an argument should only be started if you're going to resolve something through it.

ARE YOU ACTUALLY LISTENING TO WHAT THE OTHER PERSON HAS TO SAY DURING THE ROW? We generally have 50 conversations a day, and in the vast majority of them we don't really listen to what the other person is saying. Add to this the heated environment of an argument and you are not going to resolve anything.

STAY FOCUSED. One very common negative argument trait is escalation. You started rowing about the state of the kitchen, by the end of it you're discussing whether you should be together at all. Many people also subject-hop, bringing in everything they've ever rowed over. Others cross-complain: you moan about the kitchen, he complains you leave the top off the toothpaste. You say if he was home earlier he wouldn't be too tired to do the dishes. He says that if you didn't nag so much he might come home earlier. Soon the dishes are forgotten and the list of things you don't like about each other is getting longer and longer. All of these stop you focusing and if you don't focus you'll never sort anything out.

DON'T SHOUT. Don't huff; don't roll your eyes. If you don't want to argue, say so – don't do things to aggravate your partner further.

2 SEXUAL PROBLEMS

When a partner goes off sex, many people believe their relationship is over. In a culture where we find it so hard to express our emotions verbally, physical expression is often the only "proof" we have that someone cares about us – so when sexual problems occur many relationships fall into a spiral of negativity that can end them. "We believe this is the way it has to be," says Julia Cole from Relate. "Many people think that if something goes wrong with their sex life they have a fundamental flaw in their relationship. We are fed this image that everyone is having sex all the time but in real life the sex drive ebbs and flows." In fact, one 1999 UK study revealed that one-third of men and 40 per cent of women were having sexual problems. We need to understand that and understand how many factors can influence it.

These are some of the most common problems:

YOU'VE LOST INTEREST OR ENJOYMENT IN SEX

This can have a number of different causes; however, research from Keele University in the UK discovered that male lack of interest is most likely to be triggered by a physical problem, while women respond to something psychological. Sorting out the problem at the source will normally help here. Physical problems like premature ejaculation or impotence can be helped by a doctor or sometimes a sex therapist. Of the 10 per cent of women who have never had an orgasm, the majority of problems can be traced back to a psychological barrier and of these 90 per cent can be helped through therapy. If there's no real problem but you don't feel up for sex, then it might help to get to the gym. Moderate exercise has been proven to increase sexual appetite and also self-esteem. Both men and women admit they are less likely to feel like sex if they are feeling insecure about their bodies.

MISMATCHED SEXUAL PATTERNS

Considering the idea is that men and women have sex together, nature certainly conspires against us. Hormone balances mean that women are most likely to want sex in the evening while men are more likely to be aroused in the morning. What's more, male sexual peaks occur in their teens and twenties while women peak in their early to mid-thirties. A recent study showed that when thirtysomething women were just starting to feel experimental, their thirtysomething partners were wanting to become more settled in their sex lives. Add to this the fact that sexual arousal runs in hourly patterns (peaking every 80–90 minutes) and it's easy to see why we can often miss the mark. So how do you get synchronized? Touch more. As we touch someone we find attractive or love, our body produces a chemical called oxytocin. This makes us feel loved but it also makes us feel sexy – the more we get touched the more oxytocin we produce, the more we produce the more we want and the better things in your relationship get all round. If you want to synchronize your sex life and boost your closeness, touch as often as possible.

DISTRACTIONS

It sounds bizarre, but a TV in the bedroom has affected many a relationship. Kathy and Brad found their normally okay sex life pushed aside for a late-night chat show when they got a TV in the bedroom. "We'd normally make love when we went to bed some time between 10 and 12, but gradually we got into the habit of watching this one show at about 11.30. Suddenly, we were down to once a week," says 35-year-old Kathy. "At first I thought it was something wrong with me – but then I realized what was getting in the way – and the TV went." Children and lodgers can also get in the way. Check if the problems you are having could be linked to an external cause – and, if so, dejunk it!

3 AFFAIRS

Sixty per cent of husbands and 40 per cent of wives have had affairs – still not all of those marriages end in divorce. From a dejunk point of view, there are two outcomes to discovering that your partner has had a affair – leave, or stick with it but get over it. So many people who stick with a partner after infidelity say it always haunts them. They are wondering if he's going to do it again, whether the other person was better in bed than them – or if not what it was that the fling could give them that they, the partner, couldn't. Eventually they break up but they have had an extra year of heartache to deal with. So how, once you've decided to get over an affair, do you actually do it?

1 BE SURE THAT IT'S COMPLETELY OVER

If you don't know this, or you don't believe it, you can't start working it out. You have to start to trust the person again, even if it is a very different kind of trust.

2 FIND OUT WHY IT HAPPENED

There are different types of affair and looking at why this one occurred can say a lot about what the two of you need to do to get over it.

ROMANTIC AFFAIRS The most dangerous types are romantic affairs where the person has been swept away by their new love and becomes emotionally involved with that person. These situations often need counselling to rectify the damage. Not only was sex involved, but love also came into the picture and that can be very hard for the other partner to handle.

HABITUAL AFFAIRS If your partner is a habitual philanderer you obviously need to know that you are strong enough to live with that or you must leave him. Philanderers rarely change – and if they do it is with therapy.

ATTACK AFFAIRS These are aimed to create some kind of change in the main relationship in the person's life. To wake up the other partner, to exact revenge on them, or even to spur them into leaving when the affairee doesn't have the courage to end the relationship themselves.

ACCIDENTAL AFFAIRS Some affairs can be accidental – you end up with a co-worker or ex-partner.

So long as the perpetrator realizes they've done something stupid, it can be rectified. You also need to talk about what it takes to get over it – and put the changes in motion. One thing to ensure, though, is that those changes don't become one-sided. In some marriages, the person who was hurt makes all the running because they feel they have to keep their partner, that they have to do everything to make amends. In others, the person who had the affair makes all the changes while the other person looks on, feeling aggrieved. You both have to work at things – the person had the affair because something was wrong with the relationship the two of you share, so the two of you need to make it right again.

3 DON'T PROBE FOR DETAILS
You don't want to know where they went and where they had sex. It won't help you get over it and the more details you know, the more things there are that remind you of what happened.

4 SAY HOW YOU FEEL
Any kind of suppressed emotion is bad for you. Supressed emotion in a relationship can end it. Get angry, get sad, get vengeful – but get it out and move on to making things better.

Just one final note on affairs – almost as destructive as one partner having an affair is one partner constantly believing the other partner is having one or might do. Jealousy and distrust are negative emotions that you need to get rid of. In most cases they are linked to low self-esteem or pessimistic thinking. If you think jealousy is a problem in your relationship, check out the Dejunk Your Mind section which deals with low self-esteem and pessimism.

4 DISAGREEMENTS OVER CHILDREN

Whether it be how to bring them up or whether to have them at all, children are behind many of the arguments people have. Recent studies from Essex University have even shown that the chances of a marriage breaking down increase with each child. "The problem is, it's an area that's rife for disagreements because people don't think they need to discuss things before they crop up," says Julia Cole. "How you are going to deal with a crying baby, or a toddler who leaves toys all over the lounge, for example. Then the situation occurs, and in the heat of the moment you realize you disagree and things can end up in a row." Rarer, but far more serious, is not discussing areas like whether or not to have children in the first place. "Entering a relationship where the views on this differ really is a no-win situation," says Julia. "Often people discover someone doesn't want children when they are committed to the relationship and they continue thinking, 'it'll change – or I'll win them round'. When they don't, they realize they either have to live their life with one of their dreams unfulfilled – or make a break."

SO WHAT CAN YOU DO?

- Talk about things wherever possible before they happen. "Whether it is how many children you're going to have and when or what you're going to do when your children make a mess, having a solution ready will make things much easier and prevent arguments that spring from misunderstandings."

- Avoid rowing in front of the children. If something crops up, try not to let things get heated in front of the kids. "It causes problems because they don't understand why you're shouting – but it'll also cause problems because as they get older they'll realize mum and dad don't always agree about things and they can then play you off against each other."

- Look at why you make decisions. "The way we bring up our children is very much influenced by how our parents brought us up. If you and your partner were brought up in very disparate households, this can lead to disagreements." Sometimes you have to step back from your own upbringing and look at what is best for your children now.

If you are in a relationship with conflict over when, or whether, to have children, you need to assess which is going to make you unhappy: progressing in a relationship where you will always feel something is missing, or leaving that relationship for the sake of pursuing your dream of children. "It's an impossible choice because either way you get hurt, but it's a choice that has to be made," says Julia.

5 OUTSIDE INFLUENCES

"Getting the balance between home life and working life right is the biggest problem for couples in the 90s," says Julia Cole. "Working hours, changing monetary roles, discussions over who is going to take care of children are problems our parents' generation didn't have to deal with, and it's causing us problems now because we have no framework." If you think your problems are in these areas, go to the chapters dealing with time, finances and stress. Dealing with gender issues is harder. A man who has been brought up to be the breadwinner can often find it hard to come to terms with the idea that his partner is earning more than he is and, while power struggles affect both genders, women particularly find it hard to switch roles between work and home. "It's hard for any powerful person who is used to having authority at work to come home and find they have to handle a petulant four-year-old who doesn't want to eat his dinner," says Susan Quilliam. "However, men have had to deal with this for generations and have created a coping mechanism. We women on the other hand are only just working out how to handle it." So how do you handle it? "You have to learn to put your life in boxes," says Susan. "When you come home, you have to understand that the deal is different. That you may well be an excellent manager at work, but there you pay people to do what you tell them. At home, you may have to relax that control sometimes – it's more give and take than the workplace."

How to Be Successfully Single

Sometimes dejunking a relationship means you'll end up alone. Or there again you may be one of the increasing number of people who are single through choice. Unfortunately, society is set up for couples and when we see someone alone we think there must be a problem. "When I go out to dinner on my own I can see couples looking at me," says Nancy. "They either think I've been stood up or I'm really sad. The fact that I actually like dining alone won't ever cross their mind."

Being single, be it through choice or because a partner has ended a relationship with you, can be extremely hard, but by dejunking your negative attitudes it can be one of the most positive and empowering times of your life.

MAKE THIS "PLEASE YOURSELF" TIME

Being single is the one time in your life when you don't have to worry about anyone else – if you don't want to. "I love the fact that I no longer need to wash up, to watch bad television or go shopping for food on a Saturday afternoon when I'd rather be shopping for clothes," says Trisha, whose husband left her a year ago. "The first night I sat down at 8 p.m. with a bowl of cornflakes was the most liberating moment of my life for years."

DON'T START DATING AGAIN UNTIL YOU'RE READY

"As soon as I walked out on John my friends all had boyfriends' brothers for me to go out with," says Jo. "I'd been with him eight years. I'd never been alone and I wanted to enjoy it for a while." Traditionally, men want to go back to dating faster than women, but whichever gender you are take it at your own speed. "I got so fed up with being the eligible bachelor, I actually stopped going out for six months," says Aidan. "It helped me work out what I wanted from a relationship – and from myself. I had one failed marriage behind me, I didn't want to fall into another one before I knew what had happened."

DON'T LET YOURSELF GET LONELY

If you're newly single, or if you're a single in a social circle of married or coupled friends, you can feel uncomfortable relying on outside people for company, advice and support. And yes, while you shouldn't use the same people day in day out for support, a good friend won't mind you calling on them whenever you need help. Don't be afraid to ask. "When I split up with Carol, I didn't want to talk to any of my friends," says Martin. "They were in happy marriages and it didn't seem right. Also, we hadn't had that kind of relationship before, so I felt embarrassed about starting it now. There were a lot of times when I felt a mess. Recently, a friend's marriage ended and he came to me and he cried. We talked every day and I helped him through it. I didn't think any less of him and I didn't feel he was taking up my time. If only I'd realized that this was how he and my other friends might have thought about me, I'd probably have got over things much quicker."

BUT DON'T LET YOURSELF BURN OUT

At the other of the scale, you can be so busy showing *all* your friends that you're okay and having a great time that you don't look after yourself and you end up a mess. "I knew I had a problem when my boss called me into the office and asked why I had been late every day for three weeks," says Francis. "I was so tired I hadn't even noticed. I didn't want anyone to think I was depressed about me and Jamie breaking up, so I went competely the other way, but I don't think I fooled anyone. I didn't want to go home because everything there reminded me of him and I didn't want to face that. Delaying it didn't help, it just prolonged the agony."

What We Need At Different Ages

Sometimes problems in relationships occur because we have different needs at different times of our life. So here is what should you watch out for:

IN YOUR TWENTIES

You're more likely to have short-term relationships while you look for Miss/Mr Right.

WHAT YOU'RE LOOKING FOR

INTERESTS IN COMMON. What you do together is more important than what you think about things at this age.

POTENTIAL. Every person you meet could be the one, so although status and past achievements don't matter to you, ambition and the possibility that this person will commit and can make something of themselves are important.

BEING FAITHFUL. The advent of AIDS has taken integrity up to the top of the wish list for twentysomething daters.

WHAT TO WATCH OUT FOR

NOT BEING REALISTIC. The dreams you have for a relationship in your twenties are far more idealistic than at any other time of your life – watch that you don't wish for something unattainable. When it doesn't happen, you'll be even more hurt.

IN YOUR THIRTIES

You're looking for the person to settle down with – the person you can raise children with and rely on to support you physically, mentally and emotionally for potentially the rest of your life.

WHAT YOU'RE LOOKING FOR

CALMNESS. As we get into our thirties, our willingness to indulge in fiery, overemotional relationships decreases – we have too many other things to worry about to deal with dramatic partners.

COMMITMENT. You are not interested in notches in the bedpost – you want someone who will stick around.

SECURITY. Both sexes want someone who will offer a secure base both for a relationship and a home and family. This could be financially, but emotional security is equally as important.

WHAT TO WATCH FOR

ACCEPTING WHAT YOU CAN GET. This particularly applies to women in their thirties who start to fear that they may miss out on children. You start to drop your standards – but you shouldn't. While you have to get over the idea of finding a "perfect partner", you need to hold out for the perfect partner for you.

IN YOUR FORTIES

Relationships started at this time are often second relationships. As such, you're carrying emotional baggage and so you're not looking for anything that will weigh you down further. Relationships formed now are for you and to fulfil your needs.

WHAT YOU'RE LOOKING FOR

SOMEONE WHO'LL ACCEPT YOU AS YOU ARE. That includes everything that comes with you. You don't want someone who won't accept your children, your pets – or even your elderly parents. You don't want upheaval in your life.

LOYALTY. You've probably been hurt in the past and so finding someone who won't mess you around is particularly important for fortysomething lovers.

WHAT TO WATCH OUT FOR

BEING TOO SET IN YOUR WAYS. You've lived a long time on your own terms – now it's time to let someone else in. You don't want them to change you – but you may have to bend a little to let them in.

How to Leave Your Lover

We've talked about how you know that you should, but how do you actually make the break? After all, chances are you still care a little about that person.

1 BE REALISTIC ABOUT WHERE YOU'LL GO AND HOW YOU'LL SUPPORT YOURSELF

Neither finances nor accommodation are reasons to stay in a bad relationship, but if you decide to leave, ensure that the practicalities are sorted out. You're less likely to think you've made a mistake and go back if you can move on immediately – which is better for both of you.

2 DO IT ON NEUTRAL TERRITORY

This will be easier if you're not married or living together – but it's almost more important in this situation. You want to be somewhere where the other person's emotions can be contained – but not where they will embarrass themselves.

3 TAKE THE BLAME, DON'T GIVE IT
You have decided to leave. Try and tell the person why without hurting them further.

4 LEAVE AFTERWARDS
If you live together, don't expect your partner to stay in the house with you, it'll be too painful – and as you are the one making the break, it's only fair if you go for a few days. It doesn't have to be permanent, just long enough for a breather for both of you.

5 BREAK UP CLEANLY AND COMPLETELY
If you want to break up, don't suggest a trial separation. You have to make the situation clear, so the person can move on.

Summary

One in four marriages ends in divorce. We need to learn to deal with the negative and accentuate the positive in our partnerships

Don't always assume at the first sign of disagreement that the relationship is doomed and that it's a major "I'm leaving you" problem. Wherever there are two individuals, there will be be some conflict

There will be periods of change in any relationship and people also have different needs at different times in their lives. The relationship that lasts is prepared for this

No one likes every aspect of their partner. Don't strive for perfection

Action Plan

Do a relationship audit. Find out what you expect from a relationship and whether between you, you and your partner are achieving this. Ask your partner to do the same

In times of difficulty, step back from your relationship and look at outside circumstances. Are you blaming your partner for things which are going wrong in other areas of your life?

Those who make it work are those who keep communicating; it's that simple

Next time you have a discussion or argument with your partner, make sure you are really listening. There is a huge difference between listening and just keeping quiet or preparing to defend yourself while your partner speaks

If you are leaving your lover, do so decisively and absolutely

Chapter 10
Dejunk Your Social Life

YOU CAN'T CHOOSE YOUR FAMILY, but you can choose your friends. It's a famous saying, it's also a fact – so why then are so many of us not seeing the people we want to see and spending hours with people we no longer really care about?

"As human beings we need to feel loved and accepted," says life coach Eileen Mulligan. "This is particularly important if family bonds aren't strong. For most people, the more friends they have, the worthier they feel. There's a sense of security in filling our emotional bank account with lots of friends." And so, if we then start losing friends – or determining that there is something wrong with the friendships we do have – we believe something is wrong with us. Hanging on to friendships, even bad ones, stops that feeling. It's obvious that learning how to dejunk your friendships is not going to be easy. "With partners or family we believe the levels of acceptance and forgiveness are much wider. It's easier to ask for what we need and protest when we're not happy," says Eileen Mulligan. But with some friends (particularly those from whom we have grown apart) we don't feel we have that right – guilt and hurt feelings enter the mix far more intensely and also we don't feel we can cross certain boundaries. However, by not facing the truth we put ourselves and those people we are trying to protect at risk of longer-term hurt and other negative effects. If there is a problem with a friendship, it needs to be dealt with so that you can move forward – even if it means that friendship must come to an end. To look more closely at why friendships develop problems, we have to go right back to the beginning.

Why Do We Choose the Friends We Do?

Well, for starters, forget kismet, chemistry or any kind of past life experience, we make friends simply because they are there. "Friends are chosen because they fit the way our life is going when we meet them," says Eileen Mulligan. "There is an emotional payback and relevance to the friendship. You may forge a strong bond with a work colleague but if one of you moves job you may have less in common than you thought. Perhaps most of your conversations revolved around office politics; without that shared interest the relationship is less significant in your life."

The reason that this is important is that the days of us having one or two close friends who fulfilled our every need are over. Researchers are now discovering that our friendship patterns are usually based around two or three friends who are almost like family and up to 50 need-givers who can be called upon as and when we want them. Getting the mix right is vital to the health of our friendships. So how do you know if you have? "A useful exercise is to view friends as colours of the rainbow (red, orange, yellow, green, blue, indigo and violet)," says Eileen. "Some friends may have many colours, others will have just one. You can even allow for colour changes; relationships do change. As long as they stay within the spectrum, they have relevance in your life." So how does this work in practice? Basically, you look at the colours as characteristics. Let's take indigo. It can be seen as deep and brooding. It's intense and you feel you could sink into it. It absorbs and nurtures – if you have a friend who acts almost as your counsellor they go in the purple band; the yellow band, however, is sunny, it's vibrant, it lifts your spirits and makes you happy. You may not want to spend a huge amount of time in a yellow area, it can be too stimulating, but when you're there it's the best place in the world. Perhaps you have a friend you only see when you need to go out and go a bit mad – to dance, to drink, or to just be almost a teenager again. They go in the yellow band. Any friendship with a defined role in your life will fall into at least one colour – and these should also reflect how you see the relationship. Those that don't fit anywhere or that fall where you least expect them should start your dejunking antenna twitching.

When Good Friendships Go Bad

It does happen. One minute you can't see enough of a person, but suddenly they start to annoy you or bore you; you cancel meetings or make excuses to get out of seeing them. Soon you're wrapped up in a circle of lying and guilt, when you don't even understand what went wrong in the first place. The truth is, friendships don't go wrong for no reason – there are usually four main causes.

CIRCUMSTANCES CHANGE

This is the most common. If the fundamental reason we choose our friends is to fit into our lives at any one time, it's clear what can happen if our lifestyle changes. Sometimes this happens with no anguish, you just drift apart. Sometimes the other person doesn't realize why the relationship is changing, which can make the separation more difficult.

DIFFERING EXPECTATIONS

Friendships can be categorized in three ways, depending how we relate to them:

THE "FAMILY" FRIEND

These are the closest friends we have. Our support network. These are the people we go to when we want pleasure and our emotions fed. They advise us and support us as well as spending leisure time with us. They are like our extended family.

THE NETWORK

These are our day-to-day friends. Those we spend time with socially but do not necessarily interact with on a more emotional level. They may know intimate details of our lives – but they don't really know how we feel about them and they probably don't help us through any emotional crises.

THE FAIR-WEATHER FRIEND

This is normally thought of as a negative term, but it need not be. The fair-weather friend fufills a particular need in your life – but only that need. They are like the "yellow" friend we described in the rainbow exercise. If you want to have fun you call this friend, if you want to go play tennis you call this friend, but you rarely if ever see them outside that context.

So long as both parties know and understand which category they fall into, and that role is fulfilled, things work okay. But if one party has unfulfilled expectations of the relationship (perhaps they would like to move things on further, or you would like to move them down a category), problems can occur. Often, these changed expectations can follow on from circumstantial changes. You may not want to end a friendship but you no longer have so much in common and you want to downgrade them from say, network to fair-weather.

UNEXPRESSED EMOTIONS

As we explained before, the nature of being a friend can make us feel that negativity should not play a part in the relationship. When a friend upsets you, rather than confront them as you would with a partner, you brush the matter under the carpet. However, it never really goes away. The feelings nibble away at you and eventually blow up into a big argument that leads to major problems or even the end of a friendship. Or they simmer away and you gradually stop seeing the person because everything they do starts to annoy you. In fact, you can trace all those irritating little traits back to that one thing you never mentioned.

SOMETIMES WE WAKE UP

Not all friendships are good for us and if you're suffering from low self-esteem or insecurity when you meet a person you may find that you are trapped in a negative friendship. Maria discovered this with her friend Julia. "We became friends soon after I had broken up with my husband. We were work colleagues but when I was going through a very bad patch we ended up going out for a drink one evening. Julia was great. She let me talk and talk about what had happened and really made me feel good about myself. None of my other friends had really been able to do that because all of them knew Gary, my husband.

"Julia and I saw each other three or four times a week for about a year. But then things started to pick up for me; I got promoted and met a man I liked. Julia couldn't stop putting him down and if I'd talk about how well things were going at work she'd start to say things like, "Be careful, you don't want to take on too much". I'd leave our nights out feeling insecure and depressed. Gradually I began to realize that Julia didn't like success and that when I was unhappy it made her feel better about herself. She was using me as a pick-me-up for her own problems. I cut down our nights out to once a week and started making excuses to leave early. Now we don't see each other at all. It's difficult when we bump into each other at the office, but it had to be like that for me to survive." Friendships where you always play the counselling role, the victim role or where bullying or negative behaviour is a fundamental part of the deal should not be part of our lives.

So What Should You Do with a Friendship That's Not Working?

First you need to look at how important this person is in your life. Do you actually want to see them in some capacity or another, or do you think that it really is time to let them go? Good questions to ask yourself here are:

- Do you fundamentally like the person we are talking about here, or do you see them out of purely out of habit?
- Can you make the relationship work without changing your or the other person's personality?
- Do you really have nothing at all in common, or could you shift the relationship's focus? Do you share any other interests that you could use to create new roles?
- If you were in a sinking boat with all your friends in it, would this friend be one of the ten you would absolutely have to save?

If you said "yes" to even one of those questions … then there is still something there. Chances are it's not the friendship that's gone wrong it's how you conduct it and you should try at least once to save it. Obviously the more questions you answered yes to, the stronger the foundations are that will allow you to do this. Choose new roles for each other and tell the person concerned what's happening. If it's an old schoolfriend that you do like but you don't want to spend your whole time rehashing your past with, invite them to do something new. Don't just go out for a drink, actually do something to open up new experiences with them and to create new things to talk about. If you have a close friend that you feel you need to distance yourself from but don't want to break off with entirely, tell them that you're really busy at the moment so you're not going to be able to see them for the next few months. Make a date for a few months off and stick to it. If you do this but then get to the night and want to cancel, you haven't answered the above questions truthfully.

WHAT IF YOU ANSWERED "NO" TO TWO OR MORE OF THOSE QUESTIONS?

What if you start to adapt the friendship and things still don't work? Then I'm afraid it's over – and you have to make that clear. The problem is, unlike a marriage there is no established ritual for ending a friendship – it's not like you get a divorce from your old playground partner. When it comes to ending a friendship we are on unchartered ground – and often things get messy.

Instead, ending a friendship can take two approaches. The first is the subtle approach. The next three times the person approaches you to do something or to talk on the phone, say no – say you're too busy or whatever but don't do it. Don't say yes then cancel. Instead make it clear from the outset that you are putting other things first. Does this sound like a cop-out?– it's not yet. Often both parties in a friendship know there is something wrong but neither wants to be the one to make the first move. By starting the process in motion you could allow the relationship to break apart naturally. But if the person doesn't take the hint after those three attempts, you have to tell them how you feel. It won't be easy, ending a friendship is similar to breaking off a partnership but whereas we are only supposed to have one partner we are supposed to have lots of friends which makes it harder for us to face up to. Also, unless a friendship ends with a row there is likely to be some semblance of affection there (often not the case with a failed relationship) which can make breaking up so much harder to do. So what should you say?

MAKE IT CLEAR THAT YOU ARE ENDING THE FRIENDSHIP FOR GOOD Don't use phrases like "at the moment" or "right now".

EXPLAIN WHY. Unless the reason you are ending this friendship is because you've woken up to the negative way the other person is treating you, you shouldn't blame that other person. You need to make it clear that the reason is that your life and priorities have changed – not that you're rejecting the person concerned. If the reason is the other person's negative behaviour, feel free to tell them if you think they need to know. It might wake them up too.

LEAVE Don't follow up this bombshell with "so I'll see you around" or, "let's meet up in a year". Just keep in your mind that ending a friendship is like ending a relationship. The cleaner the break, the better things are in the long term.

GET OVER YOUR GUILT You will feel it but you have to push it aside. Ending a going-nowhere friendship is better than constantly telling someone you'll see them and cancelling, or carrying on until one day you have a huge row and say things that really aren't meant.

How to Make New Friends

What if the problem you are having with an existing friendship isn't that you want to end it but that you want to move things forward? Perhaps there is someone in your life with whom you would like to become better friends, or your current friends don't fulfil your needs and you want to go out and find more. When you're a child or a teenager, this isn't a problem, you just go ahead and ask them, but as we get older we seem to lose the use of our friendship skills. "The older we get, the more afraid of rejection we are," explains Susan Quilliam. "It can sometimes be easier to keep people at arm's length rather than risk being hurt."

HOW DO YOU MEET NEW PEOPLE?

GO OUT
Despite the popularity of internet buddies – and even marriages – the only way you are going to meet flesh-and-blood friends is to go out and find some. Often they are already in your life (at work, slightly outside your social circle, or partners of your partner's friends) but you just haven't made that step into friendship yet. Although it's a cliché, the best way to do this really is to join some kind of club or team that allows you to participate in something you enjoy.

ASK THEM TO DO SOMETHING NEW
Obviously, walking into a club and immediately asking people to go out for a drink will give the wrong impression – as would doing so to any work contact you've only got on well with once or twice. However, if you find you get on well with someone over a period of weeks it's worth giving that next move a try. Say you get on really well with someone you talk to on the phone at work. Your phone conversations normally involve five minutes work and fifteen minutes social chit-chat. It's obvious, therefore, that you get on with this person – so ask them if they'd like to meet for lunch or a drink. You'll know immediately if they are interested from the tone of their voice. If someone doesn't want to do something there'll be a short pause while they either pluck up the courage to say no, or think "Oh, my God, what am I going to say now?" Therefore, if someone immediately says yes and then can't find time in their diary don't assume they are fobbing you off.

CHECK OUT THEIR BODY LANGUAGE

If that's just too scary for you, then you can sound them out first. People who like you give out unconscious signs. Things to watch out for are punctuating sentences with gestures like pointing, mirroring your actions or adopting your speech patterns, turning towards you with an open stance. The more of these signs you see, the more likely it is you'll be friends.

GIVE IT TIME

Don't expect to become best friends overnight. It takes at least three years for tried and tested friendships to evolve.

AGE

Having friends is most important to us in our teenage years. This is when we make most friends and are influenced most by those around as. As we hit our twenties and early thirties, friends become less important. Partnerships begin to take the friendship role. Most of our friends are either childhood/schoolfriends or new workmates, but the person we are most likely to confide in is our partner. When we get to middle age, we are likely to have the least friends of any part of our life. Partners and children take the foreground of our emotional life – often friends take a backseat or they move away, or form lives of their own and we don't really make the effort to make new ones. The social spurt only really starts again when our families leave home and we retire. Our need for social interaction increases yet again and we search out those whom we can spend time with.

GENDER

Women generally have more close friends than men do. We also conduct our relationships with them in different ways. Men are conditioned to see their world in terms of achievement. For a friendship to be a success, you have to do things together. Women, on the other hand, see their life in terms of feeling. Just being with a friend is enough to make that relationship work.

THE SIGNS OF A GOOD FRIENDSHIP

We've talked more than once about the importance of your friendships giving you positive reinforcement, but how do you know if yours do this? Look at the following:

SHARED VALUES

These are even more important than shared interests. If you and your friend believe the same things you are more likely to withstand the changes in circumstances that can split up other partnerships.

EQUALITY

You should both get to give and take in the relationship. Even if one of you needs more at different times, your needs should be equally met over the long term.

LOYALTY

Good friends are loyal to each other. They don't do things to the other person that go against their moral code.

INTEGRITY

You should be yourself with a good friend. Good friendships have been described as like going home or that feeling you get when you take your shoes off and put your slippers on. If you can't be yourself with a person, they are not a friend, they are an acquaintance.

CONSTANCY

They should be with you through the bad times and the good times. Many people find friends can only handle one or the other – and often, it's the good things that cause the rifts. A good friend can deal with both in the best way for you.

POSITIVITY

There should be no ongoing negativity. If your friend bullies you or puts you down, this is not a good friendship it's a negative relationship and you don't need to be in it.

Dejunk Your Family

Of all the relationships in our lives, the family is the one with the most influence on who we are and what we become. It is also exceptionally likely to be the one with the most problems and is the hardest to dejunk. The old saying "blood is thicker than water" is certainly true – and as such its consistency blocks our ability to be honest, to detach and even to look rationally at things that do us harm within families. Many things can go wrong in the family dynamic – even in families that you would not think were outwardly dysfunctional – and they can affect every element of our lives.

Our parents' influence starts right from the moment we are conceived. Controversially, experts are beginning to believe that even *in utero* babies absorb their parents' feelings towards the pregnancy and that this starts to shape their attitude in development. One 1998 study from the Touch Research Institute at the University of Miami revealed that the babies of depressed mothers were born with symptoms of depressive illness including elevated stress hormones and sleeplessness. But our *in utero* experience is only the start of many years of familial conditioning that turns us into the adults that we are today. Every element of our lives is affected by this.

OUR RELATIONSHIPS
If you put people into a room and ask them, without speaking to anyone, to pick the person they feel most comfortable with, they will pick the person whose emotional upbringing was most similar to theirs.

OUR CAREERS
The majority of men choose careers that reflect the careers of their fathers. In a 1980 UK study, 62 per cent of the sons of middle managers and 58 per cent of the families of manual workers ended up in careers similar to their fathers'. As yet, women have not been established in the workplace long enough for long-term studies to take place.

OUR PERSONALITY AND THOUGHT PATTERNS
A study at the University of Michigan found that college students who had been overly teased, punched or even tickled by their siblings were more likely to be depressed, anxious and mistrusting as young adults.

EVEN OUR BODIES
A 1999 study by the Broadcasting Standards Commission found that a majority of children aged six to seventeen said the overanxiety of their parents was affecting their ability to play normally. Fear of paedophilia, increased availability of drugs and other social nasties were stopping the parents letting the children out to play – and many of them were gaining weight which they blamed on their parents. In research cited by Deanne Jade from the National Centre for Eating Disorders, families where

mothers were dieters or fathers passed negative comments on the bodies of women in the family had more body-image problems and incidence of eating disorders than other children.

As children, we absorb everything that the family we belong to offers us. And as a child we have no choice about whether this is good or bad. However, as an adult we have a choice about how it affects us. This is the key to dejunking your family. You have to deal with those areas of the relationship that affect you detrimentally. Often much of this work is done inside our heads, altering the way that our families have taught us to think about ourselves – or altering our reactions to those events. Sometimes, though, you have to talk to the people who have caused you problems in the past. When it comes to doing this with a family member it can be hard – but you should bear in mind that family members are likely to be the one set of people who will not judge what we say. They may be angry with us for a while but in most cases they will not stop loving us simply because we say what we feel.

There are exceptions, of course. The book for those whose families' problems are more involved is *On The Family* by John Bradshaw. It deals with issues of serious family trauma. Our family relationship is one of the most important areas of our life and one of the areas that can give us the most joy or the most pain. Trying to handle that alone can be extremely difficult and unless you are an incredibly strong person it's best to do it with someone who can talk you through what you are feeling and give you constructive help. As the writer Gloria Steinem once said, "It's never too late to have a happy childhood." Let dejunking help you find yours.

SO WHAT CAN WE DEJUNK?

"Every time I go home it's the same," says 37-year-old Michelle. "My mother will criticize my hair or something that I am wearing. My dad will ask me about work and if I say I'm fed up he gives me this huge lecture about how I should be grateful to have a job while my brother is unemployed. And my sister just sits there wallowing in the fact that I'm getting it in the neck again and she's perfect with her two children and part-time shop job. It's got to the stage where I go home dressed in outfits I wouldn't normally be seen dead in, and don't talk about anything except the neighbours just to keep the peace."

Michelle's situation may sound dreadful but if you ask her mother why she criticizes she'll say she didn't know that she did. If you ask her dad why he can't celebrate her success he'll tell you he is so proud of her but that he loves his son too and feels bad if he praises Michelle, when his son can't get work. What's more, her sister envies Michelle's carefree life and wishes she'd had the courage not to conform to her mum's ideal.

The problem with families is that we are too close to them to know what is really going on. Most families, despite growing up together and being bonded with the same genes, aren't actually that close. By nature we are a reserved culture, we don't like to talk about our feelings and we don't like to mess up the status quo and our family is an example of this. As we grow up, all the dynamics in the family grow up with us. We learn what the family believes is right and what it believes is wrong. What our role is in the family and what the family expects of us. The problem is, as we begin to develop our own identity, or when we meet a partner and create our own family, we can dispute some of these family ideals and conflict can occur. In the teenage years it can appear as rebellion, but as we reach adulthood, most of these niggling family nightmares manifest themselves as irritating habits that we never feel we can get away from so we just grit our teeth and bear it.

Well, you don't have to do that any more. "The most powerful thing you can do to deal with a family problem is understand where it is coming from," says British Association of Psychotherapists member John Clay. "Once you can determine the roots of a problem you can determine how you are going to handle it." And often what the things that are annoying you *really* mean is completely different from what you believe they mean.

WHAT CAUSES MOST PROBLEMS IN FAMILIES?

YOU HAVE THE SAME ARGUMENTS OVER AND OVER AGAIN

Most families have minor arguments over and over again – but rather than rolling your eyes and getting angry, seeing these squabbles for what pyschotherapists believe they are can change your image of them completely. "It's a way of reconnecting you to the family," says psychotherapist Jane Ridley. "All feuds have a positive function and that can be to remind you that you belong. It's similar to all those stories that get told year after year at family functions, a way of reconnecting you to the past."

THEY WON'T STOP CRITICIZING YOU

Jane Ridley calls this claiming behaviour. "By picking on an aspect of your physical appearance, for example, it's like a member of your family saying they still want to look after you. That they can still look after you if you need them." Okay, so you might not think it's the most positive plan, but what you have to remember is that family members (particularly parents) have a hard time when a member of the family sets up a life on their own. "It's a battle between independence and dependence," says Jane. "Little traits like this are just a way of showing that while you may be out there making your own way in the world, they haven't let you go completely."

YOU NO LONGER FIT YOUR FAMILY ROLE – BUT TRY TELLING THEM THAT

In every family we take on roles – sometimes they are defined by our place in the family, sometimes by our personality, occasionally they are even defined by our gender, but we all have them. Usually the roles revolve so that one person is not always the carer, or the bad "boy/girl", or the perfect child, but generally we have a dominant area and that is how our family relates to us. The problems occur if we then start to change that role with our family. "It upsets the status quo," says John Clay. "We are used to relating to people on a given level and if that alters we don't understand, and problems can occur." The truth is, people don't like change – because it forces them to reasses their own life. If the little brother who has always been quiet and peaceful suddenly gets all dynamic and decisive, where does that leave the brother who normally plays that role? Our family roles don't just affect us, they affect the entire dynamic of the family – which explains why they are so hard to break out of.

YOUR FAMILY "RULES" DON'T FIT THE LIFE YOU LEAD NOW

Like roles, every family has "rules"; ways they believe things should be done and beliefs they feel are right. As we grow up with these, we assume they are normal – but when we start to develop our own views and personalities, problems can occur and often families feel you are growing away from them. This is particularly relevant when sons or daughters become upwardly mobile. Their views and life experiences are different and we then try and force our own views on our family – which doesn't work either. "My entire family are moderately racist," says Richard. "They use names I don't agree with and are not tolerant of illegal immigrants. I can sort of understand it in my parents who are in their fifties but not in my brothers and sisters who are 25, 29 and 31. It used to end up in endless rows. They'd say something, I'd try and explain how bigoted they were. They'd accuse me of being a liberal – it'd go on and on and get quite nasty. In the end, I sat them down and told them that I found what they said offensive. That I wasn't going to keep repeating it but that I thought they needed to get a life – and one that was a bit more open-minded. There was a bit of sulking for a while, but they have got better. They still say things I don't approve of but a look tends to shut them up now. I might not be able to change their minds but I can make it clear to them I don't agree and that I will never agree. That I don't fit that part of the family now but it doesn't mean I'm not a member of the rest of it."

YOUR NEW FAMILY DOESN'T FIT THE OLD ONE

Our parents expect us to create a family that's exactly the same as our old one – they also expect us to deal with our new family the same way as they dealt with us. Only problem is, a family takes two people to create – and those two people have both had different influences of their own. "My mother believes that children should be seen and not heard," says Katherine. "We have hours of arguments over whether or not I should smack the kids, what time they should go to bed, etc. Kevin's family are far more liberal and I can see them getting touchy if I do tell the kids off for making a mess or something. I think Kevin and I reached a happy compromise over the children – he's lenient to the point of disobedience, I'm more inclined to snap but we moderate each other. Or at least we did until we were with our respective families and then we'd each lean to the direction of our upbringing (which completely confused the children and led to hours of rows at home). Now we make a conscious effort to remain normal with our families. At least if we develop a united front it's easier to show them we mean it – and we never ask either of them for advice about the kids!"

- **Your family doesn't respect your boundaries**
- **Having a family that is never off the phone or out of your face can be a problem with many adults – particularly those in couples.**

SO WHAT CAN YOU DO?

Well, first off, don't expect to change your family. "Not only is it the hardest method, it's also the least effective," says John Clay. Basically, it is far easier to change ourselves than it is to make others change. Again, as with concentrating on all the ways your partner loves you, try and do the same with your family and alter the dynamics.

LOOK AT WHY YOU RESPOND TO THE PROBLEMS IN THE WAY YOU DO

Do you actually want the attention that you are given? Is it almost some kind of claiming behaviour for you? Often we provoke situations with our family because they make us feel accepted – we may think they make us feel miserable, but how do we feel if they don't respond. "My mother always moans about the state of my house," says Karen. "So every time she comes I spend two hours cleaning up. Despite this, if she still doesn't spot something grubby I feel really hurt. It's like she hasn't paid any attention to me that day. Like she is too busy with my brothers or my baby. It drives me mad when she criticizes but I get really hurt if it doesn't happen."

DON'T RESPOND IN THE SAME WAY

"If something does really upset you, don't respond," says Jane Ridley. "What keeps these problems going is that there is a give and take response. If you don't react when your mother talks about your looks or your hair, you won't get so involved and the other party may even stop doing it. Just be careful, there are often a lot of underlying emotions wrapped up in these situations and you don't want to hurt someone unintentionally."

CHECK YOUR PERCEPTION

"Often the way we see a situation is very different from those around us," says Jane Ridley. "Make sure others are aware of what they are doing to you before you read too much into the interaction."

DEVELOP RELATIONSHIPS OUTSIDE THE FAMILY

So you can't talk about your job with your father, but you'd like a more mature view than most of your friends can give you. Is there a family friend who could play that role? Could you find a mentor? If you can't deal with one aspect of your life with a family member but you need their perspective, seek it elsewhere.

LEARN TO BOX

This is something that we can learn to do in every area of our life. Basically, you need to separate the skills you need to use with your family from the skills you use in other areas of your life. Okay, so you're a high-powered careerite at work, used to pushing people around and getting your own way – will it really hurt you to come home and be under the thumb of your big brother for a few hours? Michelle in the first example was using this to some extent, but to her it was a negative thing – something she had to do. Instead, again you should look at the positive. So your brother hassles you and won't let you make any decisions. So what? For once in your life, you can give your stress a rest, let someone else do the thinking. It doesn't mean you have to take his advice, just let him win. Unless any family dynamic causes you real pain and hurt, the best way to deal with it is to change your attitude to it so it doesn't bother you any more.

What Your Place In The Family Means To You

Huge amounts of research has been done into how our family affects our personality. Check out this lot and see if you agree

IF YOU'RE THE FIRST BORN YOU'RE MORE LIKELY TO BE:

- Self-confident or bossy
- Ambitious
- Responsible
- Better at speaking
- Aggressive if someone stands in your way

MIDDLE CHILDREN ARE MOST LIKELY TO BE:

- Independent
- Sociable
- Competitive
- Loners
- Low in self-esteem

ONLY CHILDREN ARE MOST LIKELY TO BE:

- Self-starting
- Serious
- Responsible
- Organized
- Hypersensitive to criticism

AND IF IT DOES CAUSE YOU PAIN?

Then deal with it. "Many of us forget that our family, particularly our parents, are adults too," says Jane Ridley. "We never relate to them on an adult to adult basis; instead we use the role we play in the family. Sometimes you need to sit a family member down and say to them. 'Look, we need to talk adult to adult. What you do upsets me. I don't like whatever it is. I need that behaviour to change,' and see what happens. Sometimes you'll be surprised at the results."

FAMILY FEUDS – HOW TO HEAL A LONG-TIME HURT

Sometimes in families, arguments blow up out of proportion and one or more members end up not speaking to each other for years. This can lead to many problems both inside the family and inside the heads of the people concerned. "I constantly felt guilty about not talking to my eldest sister," says Paul. "We hadn't spoken for six years over a fight I had had with her husband – she still didn't know that it was because I found out he was having an affair and even when things got really bad I couldn't be the one to tell her that. It really hurt my family over the years we didn't talk but I couldn't tell anyone why it had happened – someone would have told her and I didn't want that to happen.

"It got to the stage when my mum couldn't have all her grandchildren there for Christmas because she wouldn't go there if I was there, so we alternated. A year ago she split up with the husband. After three months I went round there. When she opened the door she looked completely shocked. It turned out she'd wanted to make up years ago, but her husband had told her that he'd called me and I didn't want to know. I told her the whole story. She couldn't believe we'd been so stupid – turned out she'd thought he'd been playing away. In fact, that was why they'd split up this time. We went to see my mum that afternoon together – I've never seen so many tears. Now we spend every other Saturday together. We wasted so much time on someone else's problem that we have to catch up now."

"You can never get over the problems that a feud throws up without dealing with your contribution to the problem," says Jane Ridley. "Often we use feuds as a way of not admitting our part in the problem and that may be why they keep hanging around in our heads. If you want to get over the feelings of a feud, you have to deal with the issues related to it."

SO WHAT SHOULD YOU DO?

Explore the reasons behind what's gone on. Why did this thing happen? Is that relevant now? Do you still feel the same way about the person? If the answer is "yes", you need to look at why it gives you grief. Why are you having problems getting over it? If it's because you feel you shouldn't have behaved that way, ask why – is it because you were wrong or is it because "people don't do that in your family"?

If, working through all of this, you realize that you actually don't want to be arguing with this person any longer, you need to do something about it or it'll gnaw away at you for ever. How many people only wake up to the fact that they should have made amends when it's too late? "You can face up to the fact that they may not want to make amends with you, but until you make that first approach you will not know," says Jane Ridley. "If a face-to-face meeting is too much, try another approach. A birthday card or a letter can be enough to break the ice."

Summary

Our relationships can be the most painful things in our life – or the most joyous. Dejunking your relationship can ensure that all your interactions with people are as positive as they can be.

Knowing what you want from each of the relationships in your life is they first step in getting what you want from the relationships in your life

Sometimes you have to be prepared to speak to the people in your life about what the problem is – sometimes you have to be prepared to face up to change yourself

A good relationship doesn't have to be perfect

Action Plan

Do a relationship audit. Find out who is in your life and what roles they have. Do those roles fulfil your needs? Do those that have the roles live up to them? If not, look at what you need to do to change things and start working on it

Spend today looking for the positive interactions you have with the people in your life. Don't dwell on the negative unless it is to find a solution to a problem. Do this again tomorrow – and the next day, until it becomes a natural part of your life

If there are people you want to get to know better take the first step today. If there are people whose focus in your life you would like to alter, start to do that too

Next time you get into an argument, focus. Try to make it last no more than ten minutes. Try not to raise your voice and always aim to have come up with some solutions to the problem by the end of it

Enjoy your relationships. Make them positive and make them affirming. Life's too short to waste on people who we find wanting

Chapter 11
The Total Dejunk

SOME OF YOU WILL HAVE GOT THIS FAR *and tried what I've suggested but think I still haven't answered your particular problem – how do you go about dejunking your life completely? How do you uproot and move from town to country – or to another country? How do you quit work completely? How do you pluck up the courage to end a relationship that doesn't work for you? Perhaps this has always been your dream, or perhaps now you've worked through the other practical chapters your life circumstances have changed and everything has fallen into place to make a long-held dream a reality. So how do you go about making things happen?*

Well, first you should examine exactly why you are changing. What is the real reason? When it comes to making a major life change there should only be one answer to this.

It is the Way Your Life Has to Go Now

So many people who change their life don't do it for this reason. Instead, they are reacting to outside stimuli or to boredom with the life they have now. One extremely common reason for change is to escape from something. It's also one of the worst reasons. That's not change, it's running away, and whatever problems you're trying to get away from will come with you. You should also avoid changing your life just because you want to do something you haven't done before. Just because you've never lived in the country doesn't mean it's the right direction for your life to take.

The only reason that you should fundamentally change the direction of your life should be that it's the way your life *has* to go at that time. Bob did exactly this. Seven years ago he was working in a bar in central London. "I'd had a series of dead-end jobs because what I really wanted to do was art, but for a number of reasons that just wasn't possible for me to pursue in the UK. I was living with friends in Marble Arch and had recently finished a long-term relationship. To say I was in limbo was an understatement. One day this American girl and her friend walked in. We got chatting and agreed to go out that night. It changed my life for ever – I fell in love.

"She was engaged back home, but for the next three weeks we were inseparable – she even cancelled the rest of her trip round Europe. One night, she called home and called off the engagement. The day she went home was the worst day of my life. I'd known it was coming but I hadn't really known how I'd feel. Before her plane touched the tarmac at Boston airport I had called her parents and left a message to say I was coming out. We'd discussed this but I wasn't sure. However, once she'd gone I realized she was the only thing in the world I cared about at that time and so I had to do it.

"At first it was a nightmare. I was living in a cheap hotel and walking the four miles to her parents' house every day to see her because I didn't have a car and there was no public transport. Other than when we ate at her house, I ate doughnuts because it was all I could afford. But gradually things fell into place. None of the barriers to my art study were in the US, so I applied to a college in Boston and got on to a graphic design course.

"Sabrina and I moved into a rented house and her parents and the college sponsored my immigration. I got my degree and three years ago we got married. If I hadn't gone out there to see her I'd probably still be working from bar to bar, moving house and girlfriend every six months. Everything was in place for me to move from the day Sab walked into the bar. I'd say to anyone reading this. If you really feel that without doing this thing your life can't move forward, that it might as well stop now, then go for it. I did."

SO WHAT IF YOU'RE NOT SURE?

That's a pretty strong statement I've made. Only change if it's where your life *has* to go. How do you know? Working out whether a change is right can be hard to determine – for every little voice saying "you're right", there's another one saying, "no, don't do it". Knowing the signs that say that change is right for you is fundamental to your success. Things to look for include:

PHYSICAL SYMPTOMS

Your body's normally very good at telling you when something's wrong with your life. Headache, backache, constant minor ailments like colds or skin problems are good indicators that something in your life isn't right. "And very often it's your head that needs sorting, not your body," says stress counsellor Carole Allen.

HOW LOUD IS THAT THOUGHT?

If it's screaming to be heard, constantly demanding attention – DON'T DO IT. The best changes aren't the ones that shout the loudest. "They are the ones that are always there, nibbling quietly at you," Allen explains. Forty-three-year-old Jill had dreamt of working overseas for years. "I'd sit on the train and dream about it, but it never seemed as pressing as the next payrise or promotion – then one day I applied to Voluntary Services Overseas, who place professionals in developing countries. They told me they had no places for my training at present (I worked in publishing) but that they'd keep me in mind. I almost pushed it out of my mind, but it would always come back when I was in crisis. Two years after I applied, VSO called. They had a job for me in Zimbabwe, teaching publishing. It came at a difficult time in my life. I'd just been promoted and had bought a new house, things were going well here but I knew I had to uproot and go. This dream had been part of my life for so long that if I didn't I'd always regret it. I was out there a year and I adored it. It was hard, but I got so much from it. I can't imagine how I would have felt if I'd got to 80 and hadn't done it – if I'd listened to all those other thoughts, the more immediate, instantly gratifiable ones and ignored the one thing I'd always wanted. I'd say if the dream is there day in day out, always go for it."

DO YOUR MIND AND YOUR FEELINGS AGREE?

"If they do, then it's a good thing for you to do," says counsellor Rita Cottee. "Choices that may not be right for you are the ones where you think you should do one thing but the feelings part of your head says something totally different."

WHAT'S YOUR STATE OF MIND?

The more stable and content you are, the more likely that any change you are thinking of is right for you. We've said that one of the worst reasons you can change your life is to escape problems. If you think the change you are making will solve all that's wrong in your life, chances are it's not right for you.

HOW FAR IS YOUR DREAM FROM YOUR CURRENT REALITY?

When we were talking about changing careers, Jo Ouston explained that the most successful changes were those that adapted skills you had already learned. Life changes are the same. If they are more about adapting than transforming, you are more likely to be happier and you're more likely to make things work. High expectations are one of the biggest reasons why major life changes don't work. You have to be realistic.

If you're still not sure, try testing yourself. First, check out the practical side of things. On a piece of paper, write down all the benefits the change you are hoping to make will give you; then write down everything it will cost you emotionally, financially, etc. Now score each of these out of ten – mark them ten for major cost or major benefit, one for little or no cost or benefit. Which scores more, costs or benefits? On a purely practical level, that should be your choice. Now look at things more emotionally. One technique psychologists recommend is to ask what the child you would think of the adult you. We're often very much more in touch with our true selves when we are children and by looking at what we would have thought of ourselves as we are now, we can identify what's good, bad and missing from our life. How does the decision you're going to make fit into the child's view of you? If it enhances that view, it's more likely to be the right choice for you.

So What Happens Now?

Once you have established that change is the right thing to do, you're probably only at the tip of the iceberg. Actually making that change can take a very long time. After all, change is a scary thing, no matter how sure of yourself you are. There is therefore a second rule in the dejunk changing-your-life plan. Rule number two is take the first step now.

Often you can't quite put everything in motion to take those first steps. You know what you're doing is right for you, but just what's stopping it happening? A number of factors could be the cause:

GUILT
Do you think that if you do what you want you'll upset others? Perhaps you worry how your boss will cope if you move to another company or how your best friend will feel if you tell them you're moving away. Don't. The only person that really matters here is you. You have to think about what you want

DREAMING TOO MUCH
We can spend too long thinking about what something would be like and not doing anything about it. Equally, we can spend so long weighing up the pros and cons that nothing ever gets done. Once you've made your mind up, stop thinking and start acting

OTHER PEOPLE
If you change, those around you have to change too, so they cannot subtly or not so subtly prevent you from making those first steps. Listen to what those around you are saying and watch what they are doing – is there some self-preservation going on here?

FEAR
This is the biggest change-staller there is. Yes, sometimes things go wrong when you make a change to your life, but if this is what's stalling you, have a contingency plan ready for that and then make the break. If you've really done your research and planned things well, you really don't have anything to fear

Once you've identified exactly what in your life needs to change, you need to work out how you're going to do it. If you haven't looked at the money, work or relationship sections yet, go back and follow the steps that most closely reflect your best course of action. This will help you determine how feasible the change to your life really is. Then you really need to look at the outcome of change. Where do you see yourself in five years, in ten years? Identify every step you need to make to get you there – then look at how you can make these steps. Ask is the change realistic? What financial changes would it mean? What outside support do I need? Can I get that? What are my commitments? What would happen to them? Only once you have dealt with these questions can you actually go out and make that change. But once you have, everything's in place and it's time to go out and make things happen.

Decide step one, set a date to do it, get everything in place – and go for it. From then on everything is possible. Just remember to keep planning, keep focused and keep evaluating. There's nothing worse than making your change and finding in five years you're stuck in the same rut. Life always progresses and you have to be prepared for that.

WELL, THAT'S THE END OF THE PROGRAMME. Depending how you've worked through the book, you'll either be a lot happier with your life or you'll be about to begin the dejunk process after realizing just how much potential your life holds now. Whichever method you have chosen, I hope that you enjoy the results. If you do please drop me a line c/o:

ESSENTIAL BOOKS, 7 STUCLEY PLACE, LONDON NW1 8NS

Now you have (or are beginning) your dejunked life, the real trick is to keep it that way. It can be so easy to slip back to bad habits, so you should keep auditing your life. Throughout this book there are many exercises that help you assess what's going on in your life and every so often you should run through those exercises to check your dejunk status. Perhaps make a note in your diary every six months to run through things and check how you are doing. If you keep things updated, you won't need a big dejunk ever again – and you'll be reaping the benefits for years to come.

Sometimes change doesn't come from within, instead it's a reaction to external events and if this is the case you have to look very carefully to ensure that you are making the right choice for you. Change that's spurred by a catalyst can often be a reaction to a situation that we feel we can't control – to resume control we don't try and stabilize our lives, we try and alter them. This gives us a definite sign that we have reacted, we have moved on and we have got things done. However, six months or a year down the line we realize that we jumped off the boat because we thought it was sinking – all we really needed to do was plug the leak at the bottom. Watch out if the change you are making occurs because of:

1 SOMETHING SOMEONE ELSE DOES. Your partner decides to take a job elsewhere and you have to determine whether or not to go with him – or you lose your job and have to decide what direction your life is going to take next

2 A DIFFICULT LIFE EXPERIENCE. Many people decide to change their lives after an illness or a death in thier immediate circle. Suddenly they see that life is finite and that if they don't make the most of their own life they're not going to get what they want out of it

3 FINANCIAL CHANGES. You may come into a lot of money through a pay rise, inheritance or something like a lottery win – or lose money when your job fails or through bankruptcy. Any of these will provoke change

4 OTHER CIRCUMSTANTIAL CHANGES. Having children, children leaving home, getting married or ending a relationship can also all be major triggers for change in every area of your life. It's as if when one fundamental area changes the other areas need to follow suit to keep your life in balance

5 OUTSIDE INFLUENCES. Very occasionally people will change their life after reading an inspiring story, having some kind of experience, or seeing something on television. The things moves them and they feel compelled to alter their own life in some way

Resources

Who Can Tell You More?

So you love the idea of changing your life but you want a bit more information than there is here. Well, here's where to look. All of the following contain reams of information on areas covered by this book. Some are websites that'll fill you in, some are books that you'll find helpful, some are organizations which can put you in touch with people who'll help you further and some are experts quoted in the book. These people are happy to take on clients who are trying to dejunk in their specialist areas but please remember they are professional people and charge for their time. They cannot answer individual queries without consultation and can only see people who are willing to travel to their area. Please bear this in mind before contacting them directly; it may be that there is someone much closer who can help you equally as professionally and without you having to travel between counties (or even countries).

Chapter 1: SURROUNDINGS

FURTHER READING

Clutter Control, Jeff Campbell (Robert Hale, 1997)

Dress Code, Toby Fischer-Mirkin (Clarkson Potter, 1995)

The Practical Encyclopedia of Feng Shui, Gill Hale (Lorenz, 1999)

The *Chic Simple* series, Kim Johnson Gross and Jeff Stone (Knopf)

Simplicity – Easy Ways to Simplify and Enrich Your Life, Elaine St James (Thorsons, 1997)

USEFUL WEBSITES

www.thecleanteam.com

Tips about decluttering and cleaning from Jeff Campbell and his team

www.youneedme.com

Lorraine Chalicki's insights into why we clutter and how to get out of the mess

www.organizing-solutions.net

Allison Van Norman's extremely extensive site – very good for paper shufflers

PERSONAL CONTACTS AND REFERRAL ORGANIZATIONS

Jane Clithero
Clutter
01460 234345
Clutter expert covering the whole of the UK

Allison Van Norman
 Organizing Solutions
001 415 864 6558
US clutter consultant based in San Francisco

Lorraine Chalicki
PO Box 31503,
Seattle,
WA,
USA
98103-1503
Holistic organizer based in Seattle

National Association of Professional Organisers
001 512 206 0151
Offers referrals to organizers around the UK

The Clean Team information line
001-800-717-2532
(US freephone only – calls from the UK will be charged at international rates)

The Feng Shui Association
31 Woburn Place
Brighton
BN1 9GA
For referrals to feng shui practitioners around the UK

CHAPTERS 2/3 – IMAGE/BODY

FURTHER READING

Sports Nutrition for Women, Anita Bean (A & C Black, 1995)

The Detox Diet, Elson M. Haas (Celestial Arts, 1996)

The Optimum Nutrition Bible, Patrick Holford (Piatkus, 1997)

PERSONAL CONTACTS AND REFERRAL ORGANIZATIONS
Barney Tremblay
 The Tremblay Partnership
Premier Court
31 Willowmead

Woking
Surrey GU21 3DN
01483 740407
Image consultant working mainly with corporate clients

Colour Me Beautiful
66 Abbey Business Centre,
Ingate Place,
London SW8 3NS
020 7627 5211
Nationwide network of image consultants

Virgin Cosmetics Company
0845 300 8022
Mail-order line for beauty products nationwide

Institute of Optimum Nutrition
121 Deodar Road
London SW15 2NU
Offers literature and personal nutritional consultations. Also offers postal nutrient analysis

Esther Mills – nutritionist
Lifeplan Products Limited
01455 556281
Personal advice and consultations

Get Motivated
020 7736 0402

Quitline
0800 002200
Advice on how to give up smoking

CHAPTER 4: TIME

FURTHER READING

Make Every Minute Count, Marion E. Haynes (Kogan Page, 1987)

How to Gain an Extra Hour Every Day, Ray Josephs (Thorsons, 1994)

Working Out. A Woman's Guide to Career Success, Jackie Sadek and Sheila Egan
(Arrow, 1995)

What Colour is Your Parachute? Richard Nelson Bolles (Ten Speed Press, 1999)

Life Coaching. Change Your Life in Seven Days, Eileen Mulligan (Piatkus, 1999)

The BT Flexible Working pack. Call 0800 800845 for your free copy

USEFUL WEBSITES

www.mindtools.com
Practical advice on how to save time and address working issues

CHAPTER 5: FINANCES

FURTHER READING

Get Your Finances Sorted, Mark Dalton and Geoffrey Dalton (Thorsons, 1999)

Your Money or Your Life. Transforming Your Relationship with Money and Achieving Financial Independence, Joe Dominguez and Vicki Robin (Viking, 1993)

Penny Pincher's Guide

(newsletter on how to save money)

14 Wardens Lodge

North Street

USEFUL WEBSITES

www.screentrade.co.uk.
Helps you to price things up on-line

PERSONAL CONTACTS AND REFERRAL ORGANIZATIONS
Daventry
Northants NN11 5PN
National Debtline
0121 359 8501
Helpline and information packs on getting out of debt

IFAP (Independent Financial Advice Promotion),

17–19 Emery Road
Brislington
Bristol BS4 5PF
0117 971 1177
For recommendation of your nearest financial advisers

CHAPTER 6: WORK

USEFUL WEBSITES

www.fastcompany.com

Internet career magazine full of useful tips and articles (also available in print – to subscribe, call 001-800 688 1545, international rates apply)

www.gilgordon.com

Advice on home working issues from one of the leading experts in the field

www.tca.org.uk

Advice on working from home from the UK-based teleworking organization

PERSONAL CONTACTS AND REFERRAL ORGANIZATIONS

Jo Ouston & Co

108 Nelson House

Dolphin Square

London SW1V 3NY

Career consultant

New Ways To Work

22 Northumberland Avenue

London WC2N 5AP

020 7930 3355

For information on flexible working patterns

Stephanie Denton

Denton and Company

Cincinnati, Ohio 45208

001 513 871 8800

dentonandcompany@compuserve.com

Internationally recognized organizing expert helping individuals and corporations

Teleworking Organisation

0800 616008

tca@ruralnet.org.uk

Advice and tips on setting up work from home

Chapter 7: Stress Levels

FURTHER READING

Beat Stress and Fatigue, Patrick Holford (Piatkus, 1998)

Stress Busters, Robert Holden (Thorsons, 1992)

Principles of Stress Management, Vera Peiffer (Thorsons, 1996)

PERSONAL CONTACTS AND REFERRAL ORGANIZATIONS

International Society of Professional Aromatherapists
01455 637987
Details of your nearest aromatherapist

British Wheel of Yoga
01529 306851
Details of your nearest yoga class

Chapter 8: Mind

FURTHER READING

Worry: Controlling It and Using It Wisely, Edward Hallowell (Ballantine Books, 1998)

Fear of Food, Genevieve Blais (Bloomsbury, 1995)

Happiness Now, Robert Holden (Thorsons, 1998)

SuperConfidence, Gael Lindenfield (Thorsons, 1989)

Managing Anger, Gael Lindenfield (Thorsons, 2000)

The Confidence to be Yourself (How To Boost Your Self Esteem) Dr Brian Roet (Piatkus, 1998)

Coping Successfully with Panic Attacks, Shirley Trickett (Sheldon Press, 1992)

Overcoming Guilt, Dr Windy Dryden, (Sheldon Press, 1994)

A Complete Guide to Therapy, Joel Kovel (Penguin, 1994 – out of print)

USEFUL WEBSITES

www.execpc.com/~tonyz
Tony Schirtzinger's on-line therapy site. Full of information and offers online counselling

http://mentalhelp.net/
Internet-based advice and self-help focusing on many areas of mental health and well-being

PERSONAL CONTACTS AND REFERRAL ORGANIZATIONS
National Centre for Eating Disorders
01372 469493
Referrals to counsellors specializing in problems with body image and eating disorders

Depression Alliance
PO Box 1022
SE1 7QB

First Steps to Freedom
01926 851608
Helpline dealing with phobias and other anxiety disorders – including panic attacks

British Association for Counselling
1 Regent Place
Rugby
Warwickshire
CV21 2PJ
01788 550899
Referrals to counsellors in all areas

Samaritans
Check phone book for local branch or call 08457 909090
Telephone service to help you talk about problems you may be having in any area of your life

CHAPTERS 9/10: LOVE/SOCIAL LIFE

FURTHER READING
The Relate Guide to Staying Together, Susan Quilliam (Vermillion, 1995)
Stop Arguing, Start Talking, Susan Quilliam (Vermillion, 1998)
Families and How to Survive Them, Robin Skynner and John Cleese (Cedar, 1983)
Bradshaw On: The Family, John Bradshaw (HCI, 1988)

PERSONAL CONTACTS AND REFERRAL ORGANISATIONS

RELATE
See Yellow Pages or check out their website, www.relate.com
National network of relationship counsellors

Single Again
Suite 33
10 Barleymow Passage
London W4 4PH
www.singleagain.co.uk
Organization for single people

Gingerbread
7 Sovereign Court
Sovereign Close
London E1 3HW
0800 018 4318
www.gingerbread.org.uk
Organization for lone parents

Insitute for Psychosexual Medicine
11 Chandos Street
Cavendish Square
London W1M 9DE
020 7580 0631
Offers referrals to sexual counsellors

BOOKS USED FOR STATISTICAL REFERENCE

Megatrends for Women, Patricia Aburdene & John Naisbitt (Century, 1993)

The Popcorn Report, Faith Popcorn (Arrow, 1991)

Downshifting, Polly Ghazi and Judy Jones (Coronet Books, 1997)

Simplicity, Edward de Bono (Penguin, 1999)

Social Psychology of Leisure, Michael Argyle (Penguin, 1996 – out of print)

The Tao of Sex, Health and Longevity, Daniel Reid (Simon and Schuster, 1989)

Picture Credits

notes